More Praise for
Teaching Virtues: Building Character Across the Curriculum

"In this brilliantly written, utterly practical book, the authors tell and
show teachers—and anybody with an interest in our future generations—how to build
this wise and ancient way of learning into both classroom practice and everyday life.
Help make the world a better place: read and use this book now!"
— Thom Hartmann, author of *The Last Hours of Ancient Sunlight*
and *ADD: A Different Perception*

"*Teaching Virtues* adds to our understanding of the connections between the teaching
of virtues and the practice of moral reciprocity within community.
As the book is based on the American Indians' varied and rich experience of
community, it brings a tradition of wisdom to the authors' specific recommendations
for reforming the curriculum—which is much needed at this time."
— C. A. Bowers, author of *Educating for an Ecologically
Sustainable Future* and *The Culture of Denial*

"Here is an educational approach that honors the interconnectedness of the
world and helps our young people engage it with wisdom and integrity.
The authors combine the inspiration of spirituality and ecologically
rooted indigenous traditions within the creative practices of progressive educators.
The result is a refreshing perspective on character education."
— Ron Miller, author of *What Are Schools For? Holistic Education in American
Culture* and publisher, *Paths of Learning* magazine

"Seldom do I receive manuscripts in this field with as much passion
and beautiful writing as this. I wish we could have published it."
— Don Bohl, publisher, National Professional Resources

"*Teaching Virtues* is a fundamental and welcomed change in educational approaches
to building character. It uses a meaningful context to youth rather than just
dishing out facts and hoping that kids will eventually succeed in life."
— Vine Deloria Jr., author of *Spirit and Reason: A Vine Deloria Jr. Reader*

"The authors of *Teaching Virtues: Building Character across the Curriculum*
invite the reader to think 'outside the box' as they construct an innovative
model for character, drawing from the great spiritual traditions
of First Nations people of North America."
— Larry Brendtro, director, Reclaiming Youth International
and author of *Reclaiming Youth at Risk* and *Positive Peer Culture*

Teaching Virtues

Building Character Across the Curriculum

Don Trent Jacobs
Jessica Jacobs-Spencer

with contributions from
Richard M. Jones and Edwin J. Dawson

The Scarecrow Press, Inc.
A Scarecrow Education Book
Lanham, Maryland, and London
2001

SCARECROW PRESS, INC.
A Scarecrow Education Book

Published in the United States of America
by Scarecrow Press, Inc.
4720 Boston Way, Lanham, Maryland 20706
www.scarecroweducation.com

4 Pleydell Gardens, Folkestone
Kent CT20 2DN, England

British Library Cataloguing in Publication Information Available

Library of Congress Cataloging-in-Publication Data

Jacobs, Donald Trent, 1946–
    Teaching virtues : building character across the curriculum / Don Trent
Jacobs, Jessica Jacobs-Spencer.
        p. cm. — (A Scarecrow education book)
    Includes bibliographical references.
    ISBN 0-8108-3963-6 (pbk. : alk. paper)
    1. Moral education—United States. 2. Character—Study and teaching
—United States. 3. Indians of North America—Religion. I. Jacobs-Spencer,
Jessica. II. Title. III. Series.
LC311 .J27 2001
370.11'4'0973—dc21   00-053139

♾™ The paper used in this publication meets the minimum requirements of
American National Standard for Information Sciences—Permanence of
Paper for Printed Library Materials, ANSI/NISO Z39.48-1992.
Manufactured in the United States of America.

About the cover artwork:
"Hoop dancers carrying one hoop representing the circle
of life are recorded on ancient pictographs in the Paha
Sapa (Black Hills) of South Dakota. Today, hoop dancers
from many tribes continue this tradition, adding more
hoops, perhaps to reflect that there are many circles within
the circle of life and that we can learn to balance them."
                                                — Dallas Chief Eagle

For Sage

Contents

Preface

I had learned many English words in the white man's school,
and could recite part of the Ten Commandments. I learned to eat
with a knife and fork. I also learned that a person is expected to
think with his head and not his heart, and about his money not his spirit.
— Sun Chief, Hopi, in Nabokov, *Native American Testimony*

Indigenous education enables individuals to reach completeness
by learning to . . . see things deeply . . . and to recognize and
honor the teacher of spirit within themselves and the natural world.
This is the educational legacy of indigenous people.
— Gregory Cajete, *Look to the Mountain*

Curriculum development in the postmodern era includes attention
to the wisdom embedded in Native American spirituality, for it is in the
very sacred land of the Native people that American education now finds its home.
— Patrick Slattery, *Curriculum Development in the Postmodern Era*

Our ideas about teaching virtues stem from a fundamental American Indian view that sees the universe as intimate relationships of living things that are vitally affected by attributes we call *universal virtues*. From all the noble creatures that display courage, patience, humility, generosity, or fortitude we learn about the respect and responsibility necessary to keep these intimate relationships in natural harmony.

Such a perspective is not exclusively American Indian, but by and large, schools throughout the United States have generally departed from many important indigenous values. For example, they do not have policies that see human relationships with nature as dependent and morally reciprocal. More inclined toward individualism and mechanistic structures than community or holistic processes, the dominant worldview emphasizes economic utility and consumption rather than diversity and conservation. With such a priority, moral education is not about a commitment to life and its interconnections, but is merely another vehicle for enforcing conformity on behalf of economic outcomes.

When proponents of *character education* endorse programs that segregate spiritual,[1] ethical, ecological, and moral issues from standard academic subjects, they violate authentic principles of character. By forcing compliance with certain values or by inculcating rather than cultivating virtue awareness, they teach compliance, not character.[2] They see teaching virtues as something independent from the affective aspects of moral development, such as caring or compassion. Or they relegate the traits of good personhood to the exclusive domain of a particular religion. None of these approaches does much to maintain harmonious relationships.

In this book we show how teachers, teacher candidates, parents, administrators, and students can weave awareness and a consideration of core universal virtues into every subject on a daily basis. In the same way our Indian ancestors blended ideas about courage or generosity into teaching a child to make a bow and arrow, teachers help students understand relationships between virtues and all of the subjects required in our schools. With a daily integration of virtue awareness in the curriculum, students can internalize virtues as a part of their identity and learn how this identity relates to the larger web of life.

Acknowledging that our approach to character education[3] originates from the people whose blood colors the soil of the American landscape provides a new paradigm for teaching virtues. Without this different perspective, it might be difficult to avoid the pitfalls that ultimately cause genuine character education to receive more lip service than application, cause it to take a turn in the wrong direction, cause it to become more associated with a religion than a way of life, or cause it to be overly anthropocentric. Our current educational direction does not support an authentic approach to learning virtues and content simultaneously or interactively.[4] The structures of our institutions often contradict the precepts of good character.

For example, we might talk about generosity as an aspect of fair play in competition, but in our dominant culture the importance of winning and the expectations surrounding winning can counter genuine generosity. One dimension of this is how the winner not only wins but also receives gifts, awards, and recognition for winning. From the American Indian perspective, when someone achieves success, this person is expected to give to those who helped him or her gain the success.

There was a time when American Indian elders used stories and experiences to teach virtues as a way of life. They believed that right actions kept the world from spinning out of control. Wrong actions disturbed the precarious balance of nature. By and large, the people lived in accordance with this belief. They "walked the talk." While children learned to master skills for living, they learned to cherish the virtues necessary to use the skills in a balanced way. From this came freedom, genuine respect for all relationships, an abiding love of nature, and adherence to principles of truth, generosity, courage, humility, equity, and brotherhood.[5] This contrasts with our current system of education, with its overemphasis on standardized tests, technology, and competitiveness, which provides us with more efficient ways to go backwards and arrange the world in a way that may cause us to lose our ability to experience it.

In saying this, we are not putting American Indians or their cultures on a pedestal. We know that all humans of any race, culture, or group have the same potential for greed, selfishness, wrongdoing, or stupidity, and that all people can be generous, patient, courageous, honest, persevering, and humble. However, in spite of the fact that studies of world history or world religions often exclude American Indians,[6] there is ample research revealing that indigenous societies are more likely to revere interdependence, cooperation, and reciprocity than western cultures.

For example, Research conducted at Boise State University shows that, even today, American Indian learners are influenced significantly more than non-Indian learners by the degrees to which group harmony and holistic approaches to health and spirituality exist in the learning environment.[7] The study concluded that:

> The values which produced significant differences between American Indians and non-Indians provide an interesting point of discussion. When considering which values affect socialization practice and subsequently one's approach to learning, the American Indian respondents selected discipline, group harmony, holistic approaches to health and spirituality to a greater extent than non-Indians. These values all speak to the integral aspects of one's life which communicate balance and respect and apparently affect the way in which one approaches a new learning situation.[8]

That this difference exists is revealing to us and supports the idea that there is much to learn about character education from the American Indian perspective.[9] It will allow us finally to integrate skills and virtues in a way that allows children to construct meaning and relevancy from both. To begin accomplishing this now, we offer this book as a way to begin "walking the talk."[10]

Notes

1. By *spiritual*, we mean a sacred awareness that we are all related and that all things in the seen and unseen universe are interconnected. This, of course, includes our vital relationships and interdependence on the earth and its creatures.

2. Various paths should be taken when teaching virtues to enable students to gain sound moral positions on complex issues. Students can have opportunities to wrestle with their own moral dilemmas within the framework of larger networks. Teachers guide them toward thinking through for themselves the way in which identification with virtues can affect self and others. We wish to thank Isaak Cranwell a Russian friend of one of the authors, for the phrase regarding *cultivation* versus *inculcation* of virtues.

3. This phrase can be misunderstood, misused, or even misleading. Many character education programs violate our precepts for the phrase, but we use it nonetheless. For our definition and definitions of most of the terms we use in this book, see chapter 3.

4. Alfie Kohn says that "character education rests on three ideological legs: behaviorism, conservatism, and religion" (See *Phi Delta Kappan*, February 1997 or *www.alfiekohn.org/teaching/hnttv.htm*). The American Indian perspective rests on holistic concepts that include self-determination, community, and spiritual awareness.

5. We again refer to the notion that Native American perspectives are a missing link in education renewal by quoting from *Curriculum Development in the Postmodern Era*. The editor states, "Curriculum development in the postmodern era includes attention to the wisdom embedded in Native American spirituality, for it is in the very sacred land of the native people that American education now finds its home." Similarly, acclaimed special educator and author Larry Brendtro says in his book, *Reclaiming Youth at Risk*, "Native American philosophies of child management represent what is perhaps the most effective system of positive discipline ever developed." These approaches emerged from cultures where the central purpose of life was the education and empowerment of children." Keep in mind also that there is an intrinsic relationship between moral development and civic responsibility that leads to democracy, and that our democratic ideals originated as a result of collaboration with early Indian tribes of the Iroquois confederacy.

6. Huston Smith, noted professor of world religions, did not include primal religiosity in his many works until after he retired from university life and discovered his error late in life.

7. Swisher, Spring 1994, p. 9.

8. Ibid.

9. See Don Jacobs's book, *Primal Awareness*, and Stanley Diamond's book, *The Search for the Primitive*, for supportive research. Some people do not agree with our assertion that we have much to learn from native peoples, however. For example, anthropologist James Clifton argues in his book, *The Invented Indian*, that "acknowledging anything positive in the native past is an entirely wrongheaded proposition because no genuine Indian accomplishments have ever really been substantiated." We believe this statement, unfortunate as it is, nonetheless, confirms our claim that western culture tends to acknowledge accomplishments in more materialistic terms than character education would. Living in harmony with self, others, and the environment may be the more valuable "accomplishment" in the long run.

10. In actuality, in this book we are "walking the talk" of educational reformers and character educators situated in the dominant culture. This talk reflects a sincere devotion to the goals of character education and the research that says virtues must be integrated across the curriculum. In truth, however, if we were walking the talk of American Indian cultures, we would be more radical in our lesson plan examples. Rather than using examples that represent typical state and school curriculum requirements, our lesson plans would be exclusively about ecology, activism, integrated subjects and thematic units, and field experiences, and would be community-based. However, our goal is to be sure that, at least, the reader can be effective in teaching character education across the curriculum within the systems of education that they find themselves, and our approach works with standard and more radical curricula.

Acknowledgments

We offer thanks to American Indian people across the continent. Their vision, courage, and perseverance keep hope for a better world alive for us all. We also want to thank our families, friends, and colleagues for their continuing support of our departures from the status quo. We acknowledge our students, who continue to remind us that our way of teaching honors the wisdom of our ancestors. Finally, we wish to honor the faculty of Oglala Lakota College, especially those in the education department, for their dedication to preparing future teachers to walk the good red road.

Introduction

*We have, in fact, two kinds of morality side by side: one which we
preach but do not practice, and another which we practice but seldom preach.*
— Bertrand Russell, *The Problems of Philosophy*

*Western civilization unfortunately does not link knowledge and morality
but rather it connects knowledge and power and makes them equivalent.*
— Vine DeLoria, Jr. of the Standing Rock Sioux, *www.indians.org/welker/vine.htm*

This book is the second one that we, the lead authors, have written together as a father-daughter team. Jessica was only five years old for the first one, but the subject matter is remarkably similar for both books. The first was a children's book featuring a talking rabbit named Reddie.[1] After a careless smoker burned down his forest home, Reddie found himself in the imaginary town of Loganville. A family with two first-graders in it adopted Reddie. At first they played with him outdoors, but in a few days they resumed their 30-hour-a-week habit of watching television and buying the unhealthy products touted in the advertisements.

Before long, Reddie's mission became clear. He would use his magical influence to counter misleading commercial advertisements that were enticing children to eat high-sugar foods, smoke cigarettes, and live sedentary lifestyles. He gave young readers and their parents practical ways to actualize healthier choices and encouraged community involvement in the process. Young readers began "walking the talk," and many parents even quit smoking. There were so many complaints from ad sponsors, however, that the publisher soon stopped distributing the book.

Now, more than 15 years after we wrote the book about Reddie Rabbit, one of us teaches in a high school near Marin County, California, which is among the nation's wealthiest districts,[2] and the other trains teachers on the Pine Ridge Indian Reservation in Shannon County, South Dakota, one of the poorest. We both still believe that young children have a natural inclination to live in a virtuous, balanced way. Too soon, however, they lose this balance in a world of mixed messages and "do as I say, not as I do" role models. As a result, dishonesty and selfishness unchallenged by courage and generosity wash huge gullies in the roads that lead to good character and balanced living. In the same way that technology is beginning to exceed our humanity, our education system is beginning to seduce children away from the sense of oneness with which they were born.

We have learned much since our 1981 children's book, however. We understand better what it takes to integrate a healthier approach to living and learning into our imperfect institutions. Some of these ways still call for a bit of rebellion, but most are more subtle endeavors. The slightest reference to a virtue like humility when teaching young people about poverty or disabilities in social studies or physical education can go a long way toward helping them identify with the virtue. For example, "Maybe you can run fast, but someone in a wheelchair can be equally fit. What virtue do we have when you know you are not superior to this person?" Similarly, any time we show similarities between humans and animals when teaching science, we move away from the arrogance that allows us to destroy the latter, thus humility or perhaps generosity is taught.

In *Teaching Virtues*, our mission is not too different from that of Reddie Rabbit. We believe that *effective* character education will help prevent our children's future health and happiness from being compromised by a curriculum overly concerned with consumerism, individualism, and competition. We also know that too much inspiration and not enough implementation is the current reality that describes character education in K–16 schools. Legislators pass laws to allow schools to post the Ten Commandments in hallways, a gesture that may be more about religion than virtues.[3] Schools invite Ronald McDonald to come talk about the "value of the month," but this may be more about hamburger sales than character development. State boards of education create high-stakes content standards that discourage the desire to think critically or creatively about things that truly matter.[4] This may be more about politics than improving learning.

It follows that colleges training teachers do not walk their talk either. A recent poll showed that most university deans of education strongly believe in character education as part of teacher training, but very few of their teacher preparation programs incorporate such education into the curriculum.[5] The International Center for Character Education is housed in the University of San Diego's education department. It is beginning to transfer its wisdom into the core teacher education requirements, but teacher education courses still do not reflect significantly the teachings of the Center. The story is the same at Boston University, which houses a major training center for character education. Boston University's Center for the Advancement of Ethics and Character has a mission statement, written in 1989, that includes the following statement: "The teacher is central to the entire enterprise of character education and must be selected, educated and encouraged with this mission in mind." In 1999, I was at a conference where Center director Dr. Kevin Ryan spoke. At the end of his presentation, I asked Dr. Ryan if Boston University's School of Education was committed to training its own future teachers to teach character education in accordance with the Center's well-researched guidelines.

"Embarrassingly," he said, "I have to admit the answer is no, but we are working on it."

What is worse is that colleges of education and most universities are torn by divisions on the campus, conflicting priorities, and competing interests that diminish the intellectual and social quality of education.[6] The Dalai Lama draws the picture clearly when he says: "The western educational system, while impressive in its emphasis on the development of the intellect, neglects the enhancement and development of the human heart: love, compassion and those other values that are embraced by all the cultures of the world."[7]

All this is not to say that others have not implemented some effective approaches to teaching and learning that emphasize the core universal virtues, such as courage, fortitude, patience, generosity, humility, etc. An example is the City Montessori School in Lucknow, India, the world's largest private school with more than 22,000 students. Founded in 1959, its emphasis on character education has proven effective in guiding students toward high academic skills and good character. During the outbreaks of political and religious violence throughout India in the 1990s, Lucknow was the only major city that experienced no significant problems. Many people think this is because much of the city's population graduated from the school.

There are also some good programs being implemented in American public schools. Northwest Regional Educational Laboratory's *Catalog of School Reform Models* lists more than 60 of them.[8] A few of these, like the Child Development Project, do emphasize virtues, and many others use approaches to teaching that encourage the development of good character. Some of the Basic Schools, like the Irving B. Weber Elementary School in

Iowa City or the Tiospa Zina Tribal School in Agency Village, South Dakota,[9] also weave virtues into every facet of their education. Unfortunately, successful programs are either those that have been started with the Basic School's "Four Priorities"[10] in mind from the beginning or, when character education is brought into existing schools, the programs are expensive.[11] Schoolwide buy-in does not happen often in schools that have not been chartered with the program in mind.[12] Additionally, many new character education programs are measured with standardized test scores that, as we will see in a later chapter, often contradict or overshadow character education goals.

In our emphasis on the importance of character education, we are not minimizing skill or academic mastery. We are certain that effective character education has a direct and positive relationship to high standards of academic responsibility. Research is already emerging to confirm a commonsense conclusion that there is a high correlation between good character and successful learning.[13] Respect and responsibility follow character development and are fundamental for successful learning experiences. A young person in whom such virtues as courage, patience, and fortitude are developing is significantly more likely to do what is necessary to learn. Learners are also more likely to understand the relevance of subject matter when it is associated with core universal values that define self-understanding and personal relationships. Such meaningfulness increases the intrinsic motivation to apply oneself in the learning process.

In spite of all this, there are two main arguments we continually bump into in support of *not* teaching character education beyond the concerns about time, training, and money. One comes from the educational psychologists who say virtues just cannot be taught.[14] If you jumped to the note at the end of this introduction, you see the flaw in their argument. Ineffective character education comes from trying to inculcate virtues directly as opposed to embedding them into a daily curriculum with pedagogy that involves the objectives and strategies we identify in this book.

The second argument against character education comes from the fear that someone or some group is going to force values onto students that may not be honored by the culture or family. Simply put, proper character education does not try to guide anyone toward exclusive political, cultural, religious, local, or personal values or views. It is about developing lifelong virtues that people from all walks of life believe will lead to becoming persons of good character.

It seems that just about everyone agrees on what good character is and what it looks like when someone has it.[15] Whether from ancient Greek philosophies, world religions, Bushido warrior codes, or American Indian spiritual teachings, people identify fortitude, courage, respectfulness, responsibility, honesty, generosity, caring, patience, and humility as humanity's greatest attributes.[16] These are the same traits leading to good character that have been identified by the Markkula Center for Applied Ethics at Santa Clara University; the Center for the Advancement of Ethics and Character at Boston University; the International Center for Character Education at the University of San Diego; the Institute for Global Ethics; the Council for a Parliament of the World's Religions (Council); and Oglala Lakota College.

We hope this distinction between local values and universal virtues alleviates concerns of parents, politicians, and religious leaders that schools are not the right place for character education. However, there still may be confusion about the difference between religion and the spiritual goals of character education. In an article titled, "The Spiritual in the Classroom," Paul Byers addresses the confusion that stems from implying that *spiritual* means *religious*. He writes, "Religions are particular answers to the universal human questions about the creation and meaning of life. Spiritual refers to the universal personal concern for the questions."[17] Rachael Kessler speaks of the importance of such questions in her book, *The Soul of Education*, published by the Association for Supervisors and Curriculum Developers, as do respected educators, such as Patrick Slattery, Ron Miller, Parker Palmer, Nel Noddings, John Taylor Gatto, and others.

Ultimately, true character education reflects this personal concern for the great questions about life, its wonders, and the potential of the human spirit. We agree with Horace Mann's words: "The highest and noblest office of education pertains to our moral nature" and "The common school should teach virtue before knowledge, for knowledge without virtue poses its own dangers."[18] Similarly, in *Civic Responsibility and Higher Education*,[19] the authors assert that education is the key to civic engagement, but that civic responsibility and moral development are inseparable. They add that the natural and social sciences and the humanities have a crucial role in ensuring that education does not try to separate them.

Finally, all we have to do now is to find a way to walk this good talk. We hope this book will serve to help. The preface, introduction and the first chapter in Part 1 provide psychological perspectives with which to prepare for the journey. Part 2 describes the main vehicle we use for the journey. Here we show how using a variety of pedagogical strategies can turn subject matter into significant relationships. Since teaching virtues is ultimately about relationships, a natural way to embed virtue awareness unfolds as long as intentionality remains consistent (i.e., the continual intention to include teaching virtues as a daily priority). Chapter 2 introduces the lesson plan format and the conceptual model. Chapter 3 explores the meanings of vital terminology. Chapter 4 discusses assessment strategies to help ensure you are on course.

Part 3 realizes the actual interconnections between virtues and content knowledge that bring to life all the plans for the journey. Chapters 5, 6, 7, 8, 9, and 10 address social studies, language arts, science, physical education, mathematics, and the arts. In these chapters we show how the process works to truly integrate content and character education. Part 4 offers an opportunity for profound reflection on the issues and challenges surrounding effective character education.

By the way, please note the parts of the dictionary's definition of teaching that we endorse when we use the word "teaching." Our original title was "Walking the Talk," but we changed it so people would have a better sense of the topic. Many ideas and definitions of teaching refer to "imparting knowledge," which is really not what our book is about. So here are the definitions that best describe our title reference to teaching virtues:

> **teaching** — 1c: to accustom to some action or attitude; 2: to guide the studies of;
>   4a: to instruct by precept, example or experience
>
> *(from Merriam Webster's Collegiate Dictionary, Tenth Edition, p. 1209, 1993)*

Notes

1. *Happy Exercise, An Adventure into the World of Fitness for Young Children* is now out of print. It was published in 1981 by Anderson World, former publisher of *Runner's World Magazine*. People were genuinely upset that a children's book attempted to challenge the false or misleading advertisements that convinced children (and parents) that cereal with mostly refined sugar added was a healthy way to start the day. The authors retain rights to this illustrated coloring book/story. It is available for motivating young people to live virtuous and healthy lifestyles by contacting *wahinkpe@yahoo.com*.

2. Jessica has relocated to a school in Arcata, California.

3. Chapter 13 explores the appropriateness and risks of using or mandating the Ten Commandments in classrooms for developing character.

4. We believe that it is no coincidence that the lack of progress in school reform has paralleled this absence of character education. It seems obvious that young people need virtues such as courage, fortitude, patience, humility and respect if they are to meet the challenges of learning successfully. High-stakes academic standards without them will only lead to more stress, more anger and more cheating. That educational policy makers have not made this connection makes us wonder if there is not some unconscious conspiracy afoot to maintain the status quo. In *Knowledge and Power in the Global Economy: The Politics and the Rhetoric of School Reform*, the authors suggest that such policy makers do this intentionally to ensure that the purpose of schools relates only to economic production and not necessarily to creative or critical thinking. If this is so, our challenge to implement effective character education could be greater than we imagined. And, if this is so, character education becomes even more important. Until new entrepreneurs see no virtue in imposing their will on our environment and understand that greed leads ultimately to poverty, not riches, our only reasonable choice is to cultivate respect, responsibility, and generosity in our children.

5. Jones, et al., April 1999. The situation is really worse than the research that shows that out of 600 deans polled, only 13 percent said they are satisfied with their character education efforts. In addition, those indicating satisfaction may have represented religious schools and might believe that teaching orthodox doctrine is the same as character education.

6. We have great respect for the late Ernest Boyer, the former director of the Carnegie Foundation for the Advancement of Teaching and founder of the basic school model. See his book, *College: The Undergraduate Experience in America*, p. 2.

7. Dalai Lama (Gyatso, Tenzin), Autumn 1997, p. 7.

8. Northwest Regional Education Laboratory's *Catalog of School Reform Models* can be accessed at *http://www.nwrac.org/whole-school/3-impact/9collecta.html*.

9. The vision statement is a powerful key to the success of Tiospa Zina. Every parent, administrator, teacher, and child knows the vision by heart and can define the five core virtues that are part of it. The vision statement says, "Tiospa Zina is a place where creative thinkers exhibit Ohoda, Okiciya, Tehinda, Wicake, and Waunsida. All are responsible for each child's development as sacred learners who are balanced individuals, striving to live in harmony with all Waka Tanka's creations."

10. Research from Ernest Boyer's study of successful schools led to the four priorities of the "Basic School" model. They include seeing the school as a community with a shared vision, having a curriculum that has coherence, creating a healthy climate for learning, and making a commitment to character.

11. They typically range from a low of $50,000 to a high of $250,000 a year for a three-year contract. The commonsense approach in *Teaching Virtues* has no financial expense associated with it, save for the cost of this book.

12. Sustaining schoolwide reform programs beyond the initial stage of enthusiasm is unlikely. In a study of schools that had implemented whole-school designs, RAND Corporation, a nonprofit in-

stitute that helps improve policy through research and analysis, found that after two years of working with the design, only about half the schools were implementing the design's core elements across the school. See Mark Berend's research at RAND at *http://www.rand.org/centers/ education/research.nav.html*.

13. Research as far back as 1995 is beginning to show evidence. See, for example, Lewis et al., 1995. For more recent work see *Educating for Hearts and Minds*, by Edward DeRoche and Mary Williams, 1999.

14. In the seventh edition of their text, *Educational Psychology*, the authors assert, "attempting to inculcate traits and virtues is almost totally ineffectual" (Sprinthall, Richard. [1998]. *Educational Psychology: A Developmental Approach*. New York: McGraw Hill, p. 189). In a graph titled, "Spotlight on Character Education: Boon or Boondoggle" (pp. 192–193), they cite a variety of programs, from DARE programs to build character to "packaged curriculum units" that focus on virtues, and show research indicating the failure of these approaches. Although they do not draw much attention to it, however, their graph does reveal one approach that has been proven successful. The program referred to is service-learning experiences, where students engage in a variety of helping activities in the community. The authors say this alone is ineffectual, but they admit that when accompanied by careful guided reflection, readings, and discussions, improvements in character have been demonstrated.

Their conclusions stem from a rigid adherence to Lawrence Kohlberg's (1981) developmental theories that assert that reason alone is responsible for virtuous or moral behavior. Traditional and precontact American Indian children have proven that when love, determination, and imagination are combined with reason as it relates to embracing virtues, moral development occurs much earlier than Kohlberg's research indicates.

15. Nonetheless, we strongly recommend consensus in choosing and defining the virtues that are developed in your class. This should not be a relativistic endeavor as with "values clarification," but should allow each student, after deep, age-relevant reflection, to use his or her own experience to wrestle with the meanings as you, the teacher, guide the process. See chapter 3 for our definitions of the various universal virtues.

16. It is interesting to note, however, that humility as a virtue is identified more often in far eastern philosophies and indigenous cultures than it is in Indo-European ones.

17. Byers, Spring 1992, p. 6.

18. Horace Mann originally said this in his book, *Lectures on Education* (Boston: William B. Fowler, 1845); however, we found the quotation in Amundson, Kristen J. (1991). *Teaching Values and Ethics: Problems and Solutions*. Arlington, VA: American Association of School Administrators.

19. Ehrlich, Thomas (ed.). (2000). *Civic Responsibility and Higher Education*. Phoenix, AZ: Oryx Press. This collection of articles focuses on colleges and universities.

Part 1
The Strength of the North

Chapter 1

Courage, Connectedness, and Commitment

We must lend courage to virtues and ardour to truth.
— Samuel Johnson, in Bartlett's *Familiar Quotations*

We should understand well that all things are the works
of the Great Spirit. If we understand this deeply in our hearts,
then we will have the courage to live as the Great Spirit intends.
— Black Elk, in Nabokov, *Native American Testimony*

Our main focus in this text is to show specific ways to implement a truly integrated character education program across the curriculum. Our conceptual model, Pedagogical Checklist, lesson plan illustrations, and explanations allow any teacher to teach virtues in every class almost immediately. However, the ability to walk the talk of genuine character education calls for more than these practical tools and guidelines. There are challenges beyond mere facilitation with which to reckon. To prepare you for embarking on this new journey, we offer this opening chapter.

Don's Story

In the early 1980s I was free-climbing without safety lines up a rocky cliff in Mexico. Nearly a hundred feet in the air, I found myself perched precariously on a narrow ledge. To keep from falling I had to hug the gray rock, gripping small bumps on it with my fingers. Fortunately, just an arm's length above me loomed an ideal handhold that could bring me to a safe landing. All I had to do was let go with one hand and go for it, but fear overwhelmed me. By letting go and reaching upward, I risked the false security of my current position. I leaned tightly into the rock, but my legs and fingers were weakening. I knew I was about fall to certain death, yet I did not dare to look up. Worse than this, I did not care. Falling seemed easier than reaching for the handhold. In fact, the closer I came to slipping off the ledge, the more willing I was to simply let go.

"To let go!" I said to myself. "What am I saying?"

The thought that I would prefer to just give up and fall to certain death rather than risk a slight chance of falling was sobering. It was not that I was afraid of moving into this next part of my journey, but I knew the gift of life was still mine to use. Just then a hawk screeched high above me. I looked up to see it soaring in a great arc. Somehow, it inspired me to make my move. I let go with my right hand and stretched until I had a firm hold on the outcropping that had been waiting patiently to serve me. Pulling myself to the safety of the landing, I gave thanks and reflected on a lesson I would never forget.

Jessica's Story

Dad has shared his rock-climbing experience in Mexico with many people over the years, and it continues to be a fascinating lesson about life. How many of us allow our fears to prevent us from doing what is right, even if not making the effort will lead to certain tragedy? I can relate this lesson to my first effort at teaching character education. After discussing it with Dad and studying it for a while, I could not wait to try it in my advanced algebra and geometry class with my new high school students.

I had taken the first semester of the school year off to care for my newborn son. My school never found a full-time replacement for me so the class I inherited had been taught by a variety of substitute teachers. The one who lasted the longest, seven weeks, was an inexperienced typing teacher. He was the object of constant profanities, and the students threw books, batteries, and other assorted missiles at him whenever he turned his back. Needless to say, none of the students learned any math.

This challenging situation made me even more anxious to use character education to turn the kids around. On the first day I began describing courage, generosity, patience, respect, and humility and their role in learning math. The kids giggled and acted as if I were crazy. My enthusiasm quickly faded. I had 40 weeks' worth of math to teach in 20 weeks. The kids obviously considered my ideas about character education in the math class a complete joke. And, after the first battery whizzed by my head, I felt frightened. I abandoned all efforts to look for teachable moments for embedding virtue concepts into the process of learning math.

I still continued to model the virtues the best I could, and I treated the students with respect, separating the kids from their behaviors. For this at least I was rewarded with more positive treatment than the subs had received. However, most of the students continued to do poorly in math and remained, for the most part, disrespectful to one another.

"Perhaps it would have been worse if I had stuck to my guns and embedded character education into my math instruction," I rationalized to myself. But I knew better, if only intuitively. I knew that if I had focused consistently on connections between the core virtues and the math lessons, I could have helped my students. The following year, I introduced the virtues and their role in the math classroom at the outset. By the end of the year, I observed significant improvements in math performance. Students showed a desire to learn that I had not expected. (For my master's thesis I used surveys to assess this effect, but the results were not conclusive.)

Of course, the point of my story is that I had to practice courage, perseverance, patience, and humility myself to implement the character education. I had to reach for that ledge!

Mitakuye Oyasin: "We Are All Related"

In Lakota culture, almost every prayer ends with the reminder that all things are related. Although courage and commitment are great attributes to the Lakota *oyate* (people), it is this awareness of connectedness that truly encourages the practice of the great virtues. Any society's failure to walk the talk about the importance of character education ultimately reflects the loss of this awareness. Our failures to implement character education significantly in American schools may *seem* to be about the obstacles that make it difficult, but it is not the barriers that keep us from making a commitment. We fail to commit because we forget that we are related in many ways to those things we call barriers. Forgetting this, we actually nourish our problems until they truly stifle our progress.

We are not saying that with this awareness there will be no challenges. There will most likely be people who will make it difficult for you. A poster near my desk quoting Albert Schweitzer says, "Anyone who proposes to do good must not expect people to roll stones out of the way, but must accept his lot calmly, even if they roll a few stones upon it." Such is life. We were not meant to live with such security any more than a ship was built to stay in a safe harbor. (The Seminoles have a proverb that says if you are not living near the edge you are taking up too much space.) However, it is a great truth that we get what we fear. If we worry about getting in trouble for not following a predetermined path that we know is wrong, then our worry strengthens the barriers that prevent us from leaving that path. The same is true for apprehensions about time schedules, work overloads, content area priorities, administrative mandates, parent misunderstandings, seemingly unwilling students, classroom management problems, fear of change, religious misconceptions, legal concerns, etc. We give negative power to all these things if we continue to fear them as obstacles to our mission.

In many cultures there are stories about acorns that fall to the ground and contemplate their new surroundings.[1] The ones afraid of separation from the tree keep their heads in the mud. When they begin to sprout, they roll in panic, breaking off their chance to grow big and strong. There is always one acorn, however, that feels oneness with its new surroundings. It drinks in the rain and rejoices in the appearance of its sprouts. This one, of course, grows mightily, and becomes a home for many creatures. Maybe people will say we are crazy for taking a stand for character education. But we can all take heart in remembering that every oak tree started out as a nut that stood its ground. Mitakuye Oyasin!

Taking a Stand

As we talk about standing our ground and remembering that we are all related in the same breath, the Coyote trickster gets a gleam in his eye. He knows of the trap we are unintentionally setting with our words. It is far too easy for us to take a stand *for* something by taking a stand *against* something else. To do so automatically separates us from the complex interconnections that give us the courage to truly commit. How can we understand the other side of an issue if we do this? If we do not understand the other side, we cannot know our own side well enough to endure sticking to it. How can we gain peace in our lives and continue walking our talk if we are always at war? Even the strongest of us surely will collapse on such a course.

A well-known phrase in Indian country is "*Hoka hey!* (Let's go!) Today is a good day to die!" Crazy Horse may have been the first to say this, but people still take pride in the courage and wisdom it represents. Such courage to go into battle and such willingness to fight or to die without reservation comes from knowing that our great interconnections do not end with physical death. Our mysterious invisible connections are as important as (if not more so) than our more tangible ones. A wonderful depiction of courage and commitment that comes from understanding such connections is in the movie, *A Man for All Seasons*. This is a true story about the persecution and execution of Sir Thomas More for his refusal to compromise his integrity. The following dialogue reveals the relationships among courage, virtues, an awareness of our interconnections, and the importance of taking a stand.

The scene is in a dungeon where Sir Thomas's wife and daughter are making one last appeal for him to give in and sign a document that would free him from prison, though it would compromise his principles. His daughter, Meg, speaks:

> **Meg:** I have another argument. If the state were half good, you would be hon-
> ored for your work. But the state is three-quarters bad and it's not your fault. If
> you elect to suffer for this, you elect yourself a hero. [Apparently she knows
> that such an election would generally violate her father's virtue of humility.]
> **Sir Thomas:** That's very neat, but look, Meg. If we lived in a state where virtue
> was profitable, common sense would make us saintly. But since we see that
> avarice, anger, pride and stupidity commonly profit far beyond charity, mod-
> esty, justice and thought, perhaps we must stand fast a little, even at the risk of
> being heroes.
> **Meg:** But haven't you done as much as God could reasonably want?!
> Sir Thomas: Well, finally, it isn't a matter of reason. It is a matter of love.

For us to embrace character education fully as we recommend in this book—i.e., a total commitment to modeling and teaching it across the curriculum—requires this kind of
courage and commitment, but sufficient amounts of these virtues will emerge only if we
realize that "we are all related," and if we understand that, ultimately, character education
is about love for the people, the planet, and all of God's creations.

Walking the Talk

It is unlikely that anyone will be beheaded for making virtues a life priority, as was Sir
Thomas, at least not in the United States.[2] There are other risks, however, that make it important for us to have begun this book with a chapter on courage. If there were not, our
schools would not continue to ignore the wisdom of Horace Mann, John Dewey, Herbert
Kohl, and the many others who have called and continue to call for the character education priority. Perhaps we worry about job security if we take a stand regarding the teaching of virtues. We might also risk alienating ourselves from our colleagues or friends. Parents and even children might challenge us at every turn. We could even be accused of
violating some interpretation of the constitution that relates to our bringing spirituality into
the classroom.

There are other reasons we allow our institutions to give insufficient attention to character education. Taking a stand in systems designed to enforce compliance with the status
quo can challenge the security our egos desperately defend.[3] People may not be able to
shake loose of stifling, uninvestigated beliefs that can prevent us from walking the talk of
our higher selves. We may also believe we are not worthy of teaching character because
we are not as patient, generous, humble, honest, persistent, or courageous as we feel we
should be if we are to teach it. Finally, we might believe that we simply do not know how
to teach character education.

In answer to this last concern, we offer this book and the premise that its simple guidelines are all anyone needs to be an effective character educator. As for the other concerns
and risks we have listed, we emphatically recommend one great solution. Just do it! Go for
it. Jump into it. Take a stand. Make a commitment. Nothing puts an end to fear like action
in the face of it. Besides, if you do not teach character, who will? Who is more qualified?
With awareness of our connectedness; with common sense; with sincere intentions; with
the blueprints for success outlined in the following chapters; and with the "CAT-FAWN"
mnemonic, you are well on your way to being a successful, lifelong, character educator.

The CAT-FAWN Connection

All of this said, our words might still have only a temporary effect unless *you* take critical steps to investigate assumptions that might prevent you from walking your talk. "Learning about the nature of self-deception is a key aspect of indigenous preparation for learning."[4] Many things like ambition, self-gratification, power, and old, uninvestigated programs can lead us away from our true purposes. Metacognition, or thinking about what we think, is a foundation for authentic, transformational learning. With this in mind, we close this chapter with a powerful way to assess the influences that guide your personal choices every day, choices that will keep you on track or not. We do this with mnemonic called "CAT-FAWN."[5]

CAT stands for *Concentration Activated Transformation*. It reminds us of two things about learning. One, it says that true learning is transforming. It changes us. We are not the same after the learning experience as we were before it. With such learning, it does not matter whether what we learn is true or false, helpful or hurtful. Either way it can change us and it can determine our life choices.

The second thing CAT reminds us of is that transformational learning occurs as a result of certain states of natural concentration that combine various levels of consciousness. Many learning theorists have recognized the need to reintegrate our various levels of consciousness to achieve significant learning. John Dewey considered this to be the most important of all educational considerations.[6] Indian people possess remarkable powers of concentration, especially those still living near and in collaboration with nature. This proximity to nature seems to keep the spirit sensitive to impressions not commonly felt. Understanding the power of such states of concentration, Indian societies created rituals to take positive advantage of these powers.

Teachers in our public schools sometimes use states of concentration to enhance learning. They use techniques such as repetitive exercises, guided visualizations, and dramatic role-playing to achieve transformational learning in their students.[7] Similarly, sport psychologists help their world-class athlete clients achieve transformation with simple hypnotic strategies. In these examples, concentration states are used intentionally for teaching and learning. Concentration states that influence learning are also used unintentionally by many teachers who do not recognize how their words can have lasting, negative effects on students who are in these receptive states of awareness.

FAWN reminds us that there are four major forces most responsible for creating concentrative states that lead to deep learning. It stands for Fear, Authority, Words, and Nature. These four major life forces can shape our thoughts and actions during natural states of concentration. They can propel us into CAT and cause us to learn whatever lessons are at hand. Take perceptions about authority, for example. A young child who is anxious about performing in a new situation with a teacher seen as a strong authority figure may, without notice, be programmed for life by a thoughtless comment by the teacher.

Our awareness of and beliefs about these forces determine whether the learning experience is constructive or destructive in our lives. In other words, how we view and use fear, authority, words, and nature can determine whether or not these forces lead us in a positive, healthy direction. Unfortunately, western culture generally views these forces unnaturally in contrast to the way indigenous cultures view them. Briefly, we note the differences between the two cultures as they relate to fear, authority, words, and nature.

Our dominant culture tends to regard fear as something to avoid at all costs. People want to withdraw from objects of fear and go to great lengths to ensure security, safety, and its offspring, convenience. Indian people know that fear is a stimulus for understanding our true connections. They understand that the harder we try to hide from sources of fear, the more they injure us. Our recommendation regarding fear is to use reason and intuition to determine a healthy course of action in the face of fear, then go headlong along this course into your feared situation.

As for the negative influence of authority, too often we give it where it does not belong. History is full of accounts of people who ignored their conscience to follow the directions of an authority figure. Education, however, can strengthen the power of conscience over authority. Moral reflection on choices and their source is crucial to such education. Inherent in most American Indian philosophies is the realization that we are the authors of our own lives. Our experiences, reflections, and spiritual awareness are the only sources of authority. Others are honored for sharing wisdom and experience but have no authority to determine anyone else's path. Even the greatest authority of all, God or The Great Spirit, is too mysterious for anyone to claim authority over His wisdom. In fact, when mystery is eradicated by knowledge, sacredness is violated. One should recognize that there is no absolute authority beyond that answered in your prayers and in your heart-mind-experience-reflection perspective.

Indigenous cultures are also more aware of the power of language to influence. Rudyard Kipling once said that words are mankind's most powerful drug, but too many of us have forgotten this. We allow our self-talk or the words of advertisements, radio talk show hosts,[8] politicians, or television programs to go into our psyches uninvestigated. We say that sticks and stones can break our bones but words can never hurt us, but this is untrue. Western languages also use words to label, categorize, and make permanent things that will be healthier if we recognize their fluidity and uniqueness. This is why American Indian languages are more adjective- and verb-oriented than noun-oriented. Before becoming acquainted with Indo-European people, primal societies did not use linguistic fallacies, deceptions, or artful persuasion as a source of power. Words are not supposed to freeze experience so that others cannot include their own perceptions. The map is not the territory. We suggest that you carefully reflect on the hypnotic power of all spoken words, especially those you speak to yourself. (In this we include words when used in conjunction with music, because music is also a powerful language that can lead to constructive or destructive choices.)

Finally, the unnatural relationship with the forces in FAWN reaches its peak when we come to the dominant culture's perceptions regarding nature. This happens when we see nature as something to control, avoid, or destroy. Education must revise its assumptions about nature so that we view the world in terms of living creatures rather than in terms of private property. In contrast with a culture that has separated itself from nature, American Indian cultures can help us remember our true relationship with nature. It is ultimately impossible to walk the talk of character education and virtuous living if we continue to spend more than 95 percent of our lives indoors. We believe the loss of a true focus on virtues in our world is a result of our inability to get back in touch with the vibrations of nature that make us whole. Nature reconnects us with the spiritual origins of love. We are naturally attracted to the sights, sounds, aromas, and sensations in nature. We spontaneously "love" the colors, the energy, and the beauty that fill our senses. D. H. Lawrence expresses these

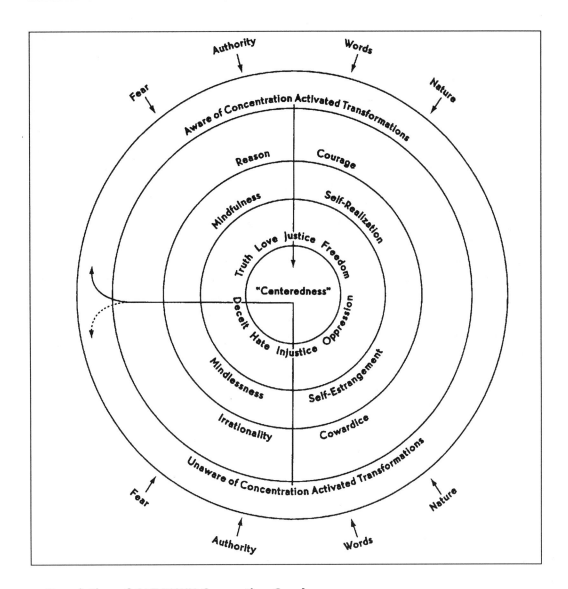

Description of CAT-FAWN Connection Graph

Fear, Authority, Words (including music), and Nature (including art and dance) are the primary influences that continually are available to trigger our concentrative mechanisms. If we are aware of their influence and interpret them appropriately, our transformations represent the application of reason and courage. Such applications keep us mindful of our surroundings and experience and allow for us to realize our individual potential. Being mindful and in the process of expressing positive potentiality actualizes our innate tendencies to seek and embrace truth, love, justice, and freedom, through which we transcend overly egocentric concerns and reach a position of centeredness that keeps us in harmony with our relationships to all things.

The opposite sequence occurs when we are unaware of how Fear, Authority, Words, and the absence of Nature transform us during concentrative states. Because these opposing forces provide a necessary tension in life and are part of the same circle as the positive forces, they also lead into the center of life. However, when we eventually and painfully reach this area, we cannot enter beyond the mountainous barriers that prevent our attainment of our center. Upon reaching the barrier, we must move directly back to the awareness half of the circle. This can also happen at any point during the previous aspects of this concentric model.*

*Printed with permission from Don Jacobs, in *Primal Awareness: A True Story of Survival, Transformation and Awakening with the Raramuri Shamans of Mexico*, Inner Traditions International.

ideas often in his writings, saying that love causes us to bleed at our roots if we are too disconnected from earth and sky.[9] When confused or frustrated, go into as natural an environment as you can find and just listen.

Keeping the CAT-FAWN connection constantly in mind helps you stay on the higher road if you use it to reflect honestly on your beliefs and actions. The metaphoric association between the lion and the fawn can also remind us about balance. The mountain lion symbolizes determination, concentration, and courage. The fawn symbolizes the virtues of innocence, sensitivity, and awareness. It also reminds us to be on guard so that these qualities do not cause us to be victims of focused intentions. Together, the cat and the fawn represent our potential for harmonious living.

A great Lakota leader named Red Cloud said that when moving camp there are some things we should take with us and some things we should leave behind. All cultures make wonderful contributions to life on this planet and its mandate for biodiversity, but too many have ignored Red Cloud's advice. This has resulted in unprecedented violence, poverty, and pollution. Not being aware of the CAT-FAWN connection causes us to take the wrong things with us into the future. It is the absence of full awareness about the relationship between unconscious learning and the major influences on it that causes us to live in disharmony. We fail to walk the talk when external hypnotic directives coming from inadequate or unnatural interpretations of fear, authority, words, and nature overshadow our inner truths.

WEEKLY EIGHT GOALS LOG

Use this form for yourself and your students. Take five minutes at the beginning of each week to fill it out for personal reflection only. Ensuring that you pay attention to these goals will provide sources of courage for staying on your path.

The Weekly Eight Goals

1. Diet: Was your diet sufficiently nutritious and balanced?

2. Exercise: Did you get enough proper physical exercise?

3. Play: Did you have sufficient play, fun, or creative activities?

4. Music: Were you involved with music, singing or chanting?

5. Love: Were love, touch, and supportive systems adequate (in giving and receiving)?

6. Nature: Did you spend enough time embracing nature?

7. Spiritual: Were you sufficiently aware of our sacred, mysterious interconnections?

8. Purpose: Is there meaningful purpose in your life allowing you opportunities to express your full, positive, mental, physical, and creative potential?

Fill in yes or no as relates to your significant involvement in each category as described above.

Week	Diet	Exercise	Play	Music	Love	Nature	Spiritual Awareness	Purpose
1								
2								
3								
4								
5								
6								
7								
8								
9								
10								
11								
12								
13								
14								
15								
16								

UNIVERSAL VIRTUES APPLICATION LOG

Fill in yes or no for your most significant expression/demonstration of each during the week (for teachers, administrators, and students to do privately). Allow five minutes at the beginning of each week.

Week	Courage	Patience	Fortitude	Generosity	Humility	Honesty	Respect	Responsibility
1								
2								
3								
4								
5								
6								
7								
8								
9								
10								
11								
12								
13								
14								
15								
16								

Faculty Reminders for Teaching All Classes

- Open class with a quiet minute followed by a nondenominational prayer asking for help in gaining knowledge, wisdom, and good character and offering appreciation. Let students know they may address any entity or person they choose with this prayer.
- Be aware of opportunities for relating virtues and personal relevance to content objectives throughout the class whenever possible.
- Practice and encourage critical thinking during the class.
- Address multiple intelligences as often as possible, including ecological awareness.
- Give homework that involves community, service-learning, or social activism as often as is reasonable.
- Ensure that content objectives align with syllabus.
- Allow time for you and students to complete the Eight Goals Log and the Universal Virtues Application Log at beginning of class.
- When appropriate, offer reminders about the contributions of the various cultures that are represented in your classroom.

Questions for Student Teachers

1. Explain how different ways of interpreting or relating to the four influences in FAWN can affect the quality of the choices we make in life.
2. Offer some examples of how certain states of awareness can make people hyper-suggestible to the words of an authority figure.
3. Identify some issues in current education systems that might make teaching virtues across the curriculum difficult.
4. Courage to face risks to physical safety is just one kind of courage. What other kinds of courage can you name?
5. How does your idea of spirituality relate to a willingness to commit to integrating virtue education into your classes?

Notes

1. The Council for Global Education (*www.globaleducation.org*) publishes a wonderful series of booklets that provide parents and teachers with a complete presentation process for helping young children explore, experience, and express core beliefs and behaviors relating to assertiveness, caring, courage, creativity, forgiveness, honesty, kindness, loyalty, peacefulness, respect, responsibility, self-discipline, tolerance, trust, and unity. The one on courage uses a story about two acorns. These can be ordered by contacting the Council at 202-496-9780.

2. We are not so sure that people who make virtues a life priority still do not pay a serious price, however. People who speak about democratic values and compassion are still punished in many countries. People who cherish individual rights of humans and animals are similarly subject to great sanctions.

3. In Robert Sternberg's book, *Thinking Styles*, he demonstrates that the single most powerful reason for success in most businesses, industries, and universities relates to compliance with the authority figures.

4. Cajite, 1994, p. 225.

5. The full story of how the CAT-FAWN connection concept came into being, and a more thorough explanation of how it relates to learning, can be found in *Primal Awareness: A True Story of Survival, Transformation and Awakening with the Raramuri Shamans of Mexico.*

6. Dewey, 1930, pp. 34–46. When we think of a failure to walk the talk in education we think of how most of John Dewey's wonderful and correct ideas about education are still not being implemented.

7. Concerns about using meditation and visualization techniques by teaching professionals generally are unwarranted. Although abreactions in students are possible, they are extremely rare. Such exercises are done for positive learning, and no one has ever been hurt by speaking positively to anyone in trance states. Much more damage is done by teachers in position of authority who do not realize the hypnotic power of negative words. For more on this subject, see the book, *Patient Communication* on the use of hypnosis in medical emergencies, or the video, *Emergency Hypnosis.*

8. The book, *The Bum's Rush: The Selling of Environmental Backlash*, exposes the misleading rhetoric of radio talk show host, Rush Limbaugh, and is used as a critical thinking text in a number of universities. It shows how powerful words can be in shaping national policy.

9. See, for example, D. H. Lawrence's *Studies in Classical American Literature*, 1971.

Part 2
The Enlightenment of the East

Chapter 2

Blueprints for Success

*By lifting our vision, the petty quarrels of our daily existence will be overcome by
a view of our future, and then our communities will emerge as sacred places.*
— Vine Deloria, Jr. (Lakota), in *American Indians, American Justice*, 1983

If you can draw it, you can do it.
— Walt Disney (from an old Disneyland brochure)

In the last chapter, we shared ways to help you sustain your commitment to character education across the curriculum and we focused on one of the most important virtues, courage. In this chapter, we introduce specific guidelines for our approach to the implementation of your character education program. These relate to professional vision and mission statements; a conceptual model; the Pedagogy and Procedures Checklist; and lesson plan format and examples that we will be using in subsequent chapters. We also touch on assessments here, though we devote an entire chapter to this subject later.

Vision and Mission Statements

We recommend that your first map for a successful voyage into character education take the form of vision and mission statements. Ideally, your school would create one or modify its existing one to address the character education priority. Whether or not this happens, your mission will be served well if you and your class write both a vision statement and a mission statement relating to the teaching of the virtues across the curriculum.

Your vision statement will be most effective if:

- It is simply put and easy to remember.
- It inspires people.
- It is impossible to reach or measure conclusively.
- Everyone agrees with it.
- It contributes to making the world a better place.

The mission statement reflects more measurable objectives that point toward this vision. In it you can list or describe aspects of your character education vision that you and the class will do daily. You can include whatever details you and your students feel will help everyone stay on track. Your vision should be compatible, of course, with that of your school. If there is a problem with congruency here, a grand opportunity for reconsidering the school's vision may emerge.

Success of your program is correlated directly to how often you and your students refer to the vision and mission statements. Many organizations have wonderful visions, but no one knows what they are. Or, if they know what the vision is, day-to-day decisions or rationales for choices do not reflect the vision. At the end of this chapter, we offer a Weekly Goals Log and a Universal Virtues Application Log to help with remembering to do the things that are important for us to do. These logs, or similar ones designed to fit your unique goals and objectives, may keep you and the students in line with your vision statement.

The Conceptual Model

The illustration on the facing page that attempts to conceptualize our model for character education. Do not be unsettled by what may seem at first to be very complex. Good character education recognizes many interconnections. (For definitions of all terms, see chapter 3.)

Once understood, however, these interconnections seem natural to the process of teaching virtues across the curriculum. By becoming familiar with the model, you will find it to be a useful tool that will allow character education to emerge naturally and effectively in your class. (Note: In the following chapter we describe the meanings of the words, phrases, and terms used in the model and in the Pedagogy and Procedures Checklist.)

The first thing to notice in the model is that the inner circles are encompassed by a larger one representing the concept of spirituality, defined as "a sacred realization of interconnectedness with all in the seen and unseen realms." Spirituality pervades the entire process of learning that leads to good character.[1] Knowledge ultimately is always connected to our spiritual, ecological, and intra- and interpersonal relationships. However, the overly anthropocentric assumptions of our current culture cause us to forget this fact, even when we use collaborative models for our teaching. We hope that our use of this idea and understanding of spirituality will prevent such an error.

In each of the seven circles, successful learning means understanding that all of life is interconnected, albeit sometimes in mysterious ways. As we grow in character, we gain in this spiritual awareness, and in so doing become more full of compassion, love, and caring. We then circle back to learning opportunities from which we spring to even higher degrees of this understanding. Thus, character is ever evolving and requires a revisiting of the virtues, skills, and methods of learning that are listed.

Since the outer circle surrounds this evolution toward character, we may infer that spirituality has no beginning or ending. This implies that spiritual awareness is not at the end of a linear upward climb. It already exists in our consciousness at birth, even before we participate in life's various learning experiences. In American Indian cultures, this sacred aspect of the child is nurtured from birth so that the sense of interconnections colors all of the person's subsequent learning.

The four spheres at the bottom of the model (experience, inner skills, external skills, and virtues) are joined together within a circle that represents pedagogy. By this term we mean all the ways that life and our many teachers teach us. We identify 31 strategies or objectives that open doors for integrated teaching of content and character. Many of these strategies are well known from school reform rhetoric and holistic education journals. They also represent ideas about how indigenous people learned how to survive and contribute to their society.

As pedagogy brings into play the four circles it embraces, it fosters respect and wisdom, which lead to good character. Good character, in our interpretation, exists when someone has both integrity and a sense of peacefulness. (In Lakota, this sense of peacefulness is referred to as *wolakota*.) Thus, pedagogy is the engine for the continuing cycle of these interactions among Experience, The Five Inner Skills, The Six Virtues, and The Three External Skills, which are interdependent in this learning process.

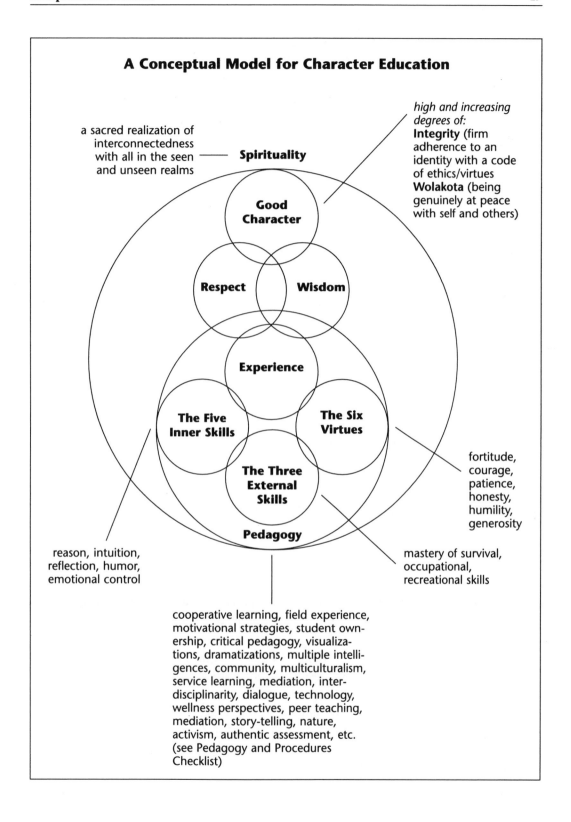

A Conceptual Model for Character Education

a sacred realization of interconnectedness with all in the seen and unseen realms — **Spirituality**

high and increasing degrees of:
Integrity (firm adherence to an identity with a code of ethics/virtues
Wolakota (being genuinely at peace with self and others)

Good Character

Respect   **Wisdom**

Experience

The Five Inner Skills   **The Six Virtues**

The Three External Skills

Pedagogy

fortitude, courage, patience, honesty, humility, generosity

reason, intuition, reflection, humor, emotional control

mastery of survival, occupational, recreational skills

cooperative learning, field experience, motivational strategies, student ownership, critical pedagogy, visualizations, dramatizations, multiple intelligences, community, multiculturalism, service learning, mediation, interdisciplinarity, dialogue, technology, wellness perspectives, peer teaching, mediation, story-telling, nature, activism, authentic assessment, etc. (see Pedagogy and Procedures Checklist)

From the cycle, students learn to embrace respectfulness and wisdom. As wisdom and respect are applied and experienced, responsible behavior emerges. The sincere love of this way of life creates ever higher degrees of good character. As this ever-evolving, ever-spiraling processes continues, children realize more and more how interconnected we all are, which in turns helps us to rediscover our spirituality.

If this model no longer appears complex to you, it may now seem idealistic. Can a sincere love of this way of life evolve? If this cycle of connections is revived and practiced in our schools, will children truly realize their bond with all parts of life and their unique role in it? We know this can happen, from our combined experience as classroom teachers, from work with at-risk youth, and from oral histories of many indigenous cultures. It will not happen over night, but the cycle we describe can become a reality with all of our children if we give it a chance.

Lesson Plans for Integrating Character Education into the Content Areas

A major reason for the lack of character education in our schools is that, with few exceptions in social studies or literature coursework, virtue training has been separated from learning content. There has been no unifying format for combining all subjects with the virtues. There are hundreds of sample lesson plans for most every academic subject available on the Internet. There are also some for character education, but few of these do what the research says must happen if character education is to be successful—that is, consistently weave character education into math, science, social studies, physical education, and language arts.[2]

Fortunately, with our approach you do not have to discard lesson plans you already have. You simply can revisit your original lesson plan with an additional intention to include character development. You also may want to increase the variety of teaching strategies used to implement your old plan to increase opportunities to embed related virtues. Each lesson plan model we present incorporates a number of the most recommended strategies for effective education[3] and the five major thinking skills depicted in the conceptual model. It should not be a surprise that the pedagogical strategies that work for successful learning are the same as those that work for character education.

Note that these strategies tend to make learning relevant to real life. They make it easy and natural to teach the universally recognized virtues that only make sense in real-life relationships. They set the stage for problem-based approaches to studying content. For example, team-learning strategies automatically afford opportunities for learning about respect because of the actual interactions with others they require. Critical thinking exercises in themselves bring courage issues into play when they are about meaningful questions. Service learning can awaken feelings of generosity because generosity is a fundamental aspect of helping others. Field experiences often call for patience because we never know what obstacles the real world may throw in front of us. Mediation is a natural environment for learning humility, etc. In other words, these teaching strategies naturally make it easy to embed ideas about virtues into every subject because any such holistic approach to education cannot avoid issues relating to virtues.[4]

We believe character education is a way for us all to help turn the tide of violence, disrespect, alienation, inequity, ecological degradation, corruption, and unhappiness in our communities. It can help us as teachers with efforts to encourage the development of new patterns of thinking, feeling, willing, and behaving in ways that relate to right and wrong, justice and equity. This is why lesson plans for effective character development cannot be separate from academic lesson plans. They must always meet both academic and character objectives. This means that the teaching of the core virtues must be as much a part of arithmetic as are numbers, as much a part of reading as are words, as much a part of history as are dates, as much a part of science as are formulas, and as much about physical education as is nutrition.

The lesson plans in subsequent chapters are only examples. You can use them to modify your own lesson plans or to invent entirely new ones. Either way, we think you will find the effort surprisingly rewarding and fun. And, once your students get used to hearing about virtues at times other than when they are not displaying them (and are too defensive to learn positively about them), they will help you identify and use character education opportunities.

Basic Requirements for a Character Education Lesson Plan

In his book, *Basic Skills*, Herbert Kohl reminds us that a basic skill is one that provides a strength that enables a certain quality of life to be supported.[5] To know what a basic skill is, he says, we must first ask what kind of adults do we want our children to become, and do we want the children of the future to live in a healthy, just, compassionate, and democratic society. For Kohl, there are four basic, interrelated goals that emerge from this perspective:

- Learning to acquire, organize, and analyze information.
- Learning how to access resources and have command over them.
- Learning how to act effectively personally and with others.
- Learning how to renew oneself, be a source of renewal to others, and contribute to sustaining and renewing the earth as well.[6]

These broad goals define our purpose for education in general and make obvious the need to combine character education with content education. To refine these goals into lesson plan objectives that serve this complementary relationship between character and academics, we borrow from Rusnak's work[7] and we suggest that all lesson plans reflect:

- *Responsible action.* The lesson plan must allow students to confront meaningful questions in the school and community, propose imaginative solutions, and become involved in activities and actions to implement the solutions.
- *Interaction.* The lesson plan must deal with real ethical issues in a practical and relevant manner with peers, teachers, and the community.
- *Integration.* The consistency, enthusiasm, and relevancy should lead to developing a strong sense of identity with the character traits in each student.
- *Consistency.* Pedagogy should emphasize continual support of students to act consistently with their ethics (virtues) in all settings and situations.

These goals and objectives boil down to simple questions that should guide the objectives of our lesson plans and thematic units as they relate to the core virtues:

- What are the most important things to be learned in the lesson?
- What virtues underpin the lesson?
- What virtues are needed to experience real-world success in areas related to the academic subject?
- How are the virtues studied demonstrated in the learners' lives?
- Which virtues will students have an opportunity to practice during the lesson or homework assignment?
- What activities and future actions will promote the virtues?

The Pedagogy and Procedures Checklist

To help ensure that the above goals, objectives, and questions are included in each thematic unit, we offer a checklist to use for each lesson or unit. Using as many as you can will automatically provide numerous natural opportunities for teaching virtues. You and your class just have to maintain the intention to do so. Each technique or strategy does not have to be used daily, but ideally each should be addressed within the week. At first this may seem a difficult task. However, as you will see in our examples, it is surprisingly easy to bring as many as ten or more into each lesson. Before long, these state-of-the-art approaches to learning are no longer sitting on the shelf in textbooks, and we suddenly find ourselves walking the talk of character education.

When creating your own lesson plans after reviewing our models, use the Pedagogy and Procedures Checklist that follows with each lesson plan to help ensure you are indeed implementing these proven approaches to learning that will lead to successful character education. Think of it as a things-to-do list for your classes. Check the day you used the strategy on the checklist itself, then reference the number associated with a particular strategy in your lesson plan when you refer to it.

Since the six virtues are not listed in the pedagogy checklist, to remember them you may find it useful to have the "Conceptual Model" handy, also, or, better yet, have the virtues or the model posted in a conspicuous place in your class. (*Jessica:* In one of my classrooms, the virtues listed on the blackboard were the only thing the janitor did not erase every evening.) Following the advice of the International Center for Character Education, we strongly recommend that you allow your class or guide it, depending on the grade level, to take ownership of the virtues, even if the students select other ones that meet the requirements discussed in the next chapter. This happens when they come to a consensus about the most important ones. Inevitably, they will arrive at ones the same as or similar to the six listed in the conceptual model. If they are slightly different, use the ones they selected. Using the model and the pedagogical checklist, teaching character will soon be like falling off a log, and you may wonder where we lost the common sense to implement it long ago.

We also suggest that when you do see a chance to teach one of our core universal virtues (or one you and your class have selected) as you prepare your own lesson plans, write the virtue and how you will refer to it, then underline this narrative in your lesson plan. This will keep your intentional focus on the virtues from getting lost in the content knowledge emphasis. You also should note any opportunities that arise spontaneously while you are teaching. In this way, you can look back in the plan and see how, how often, and when you taught a virtue.

PEDAGOGY AND PROCEDURES CHECKLIST

(Note that the inner skills, the multiple intelligences,[8] and the various teaching strategies are all combined in this checklist. Use chapter 3 for clarification of terms and strategies.)

Teacher's Name _____

Subject _____

Thematic Unit _____

Grade Level _____

Date Last Modified _____

Directions: Refer to this list to ensure that you use all or most of the approaches one or more times during the unit while creating and implementing your lesson plan. Check which days you used the particular approach.

	Day 1	**Day 2**	**Day 3**	**Day 4**
1. Cooperative learning				
2. Field experience				
3. Intrinsic motivational strategy				
4. Extrinsic motivational strategy				
5. Student ownership of subject matter				
6. Critical thinking exercises				
7. Intuitive exercises				
8. Visualizations				
9. Dramatizations				
10. Emotional management opportunity				
11. Musical orientation				
12. Logical orientation				
13. Spatial orientation				
14. Linguistic orientation				
15. Kinesthetic orientation				
16. Interpersonal orientation				
17. Intrapersonal orientation				
18. Nature orientation				
19. Community involvement				
20. Multicultural aspect				
21. Service-learning activity				
22. Interdisciplinary connection				
23. Dialogue opportunity				
24. Use of technology				
25. Use of humor				
26. Reference to wellness/fitness				
27. Peer teaching				
28. Mediation				
29. Story-telling				
30. Contribution to school environment				
31. Activism opportunity				

Again, at first you might think it overwhelming to use all or most of these regularly for thematic units of four or five days. However, as you will see, it is easier than you think. Many of our Oglala Lakota College student teachers manage to use all of them in a four-day unit, with numerous repeats. You probably already use many of them in your classroom. Some can be accommodated with homework. No doubt your four or five hours of instruction will be jam-packed and dynamic, but, well, isn't that how a day at school should be? **The point is that the more of these you use along with the intention to build good character and spiritual/ecological awareness, the easier it will be to find natural opportunities to do so within the daily curriculum. Intentionality + a variety of good teaching strategies = natural opportunities for teaching virtues.**

Lesson Plan Structure

The lesson plan format used here is designed to address these important ingredients for effective character education. However, teachers should feel free to use their own favorite formats as long as they include the key elements from both this format and the checklist. Whether the lesson plan fits a particular format is not as important as whether it actually describes what you want and what you have determined is the best route to your expected goal. The following format is used for all the lesson plans that follow:

1. Title Information: This section titles your lesson plan or four to five-day thematic unit and lists preliminary basic information.
   - Your name (optional but useful if you are training teachers)
   - The grade level of students
   - The specific subject matter *and* virtue(s) to be addressed—e.g., science (biology), *and* courage and caring
   - Official Content Standard Addressed. This helps ensure that your creativity and innovations will not cause you to forget about state or national standards goals and objectives—e.g., "Understand basic functions and characteristics of animals." (South Dakota Teaching Standards for 3rd Grade)
   - How much time you intend to devote to the lesson
2. Opening Question: An interesting and challenging question that inspires students to explore the lesson. This also helps you focus on where you are going from the beginning. For example: A science lesson plan about elements might be called, "What are we made of?" For introducing the virtue, *courage*, a question might be, "Was courage of any kind required to discover what we are made of?"
3. Prerequisite Skills and/or Knowledge: State what you think the students must know or be able to do to be successful with the lesson. List a few specifics here. For example, for an academic subject: (a) Students should know how to use the index in our textbook. (b) Students should be able to define the word, *element*. For example, for a virtue: (a) Students are reminded that we are all made of the same elements and that all living things share these elements to bring spirituality into the discussion. (b) Students should understand various kinds of courage—i.e., the courage to stand up for what you believe in, the courage to suffer persecution, the courage to help others, etc.
4. Resources and Materials: State the specific resources you plan on using—e.g., (academic) (a) bowl of saltwater and bucket of dirt. (b) Invite Mr. Denning from the zoo.

(c) Computer software program, "What are we made of?" (Character) (d) photo of Nobel prize winner, Dr. Marvin Berman, and a biographical sketch about his persecution in Germany

- The Learning Goals: What goal is likely to be achieved down the road as a result of lessons like this one? Ideally the lesson will be relevant to the lives of your students, but it is helpful for everyone to want this goal for the future. To bring real-life experience into the equation ask, How does the lesson help students understand and experience their environment in healthy ways? Remember, our goal is to implement school renewal philosophy that does not continue the fragmented learning sessions that are usual in classrooms. For example, for an academic subject: "The goal is for the students to learn how all things are related."

    In these lessons, the goals relate to both the academic goal *and* the character development goal. However, since opportunities to teach character emerge naturally while you are writing the lesson (and not necessarily before), you generally will not be able to write down the character goal until *after* you have written the lesson plan. For example, for a character subject: "The goal is to understand the role courage plays in the discovery process."

5. The Specific Objectives: What exactly do you want the students to have learned when the lesson is over? An academic example is: "The student will be able to identify four basic elements that human beings, animals, and seawater are made of." A character example is: "The student will be able to describe, in writing, art, music, why Dr. Einstein needed courage for his research." Again, unless you already know which virtues you want to insert into the lesson, the specific character objectives likely will not emerge until after you have written the lesson plan and you reviewed the virtue teaching opportunities that naturally emerged. Use a variety of performance-based assessments to help the children gain the wisdom you want them to.

6. Instructional Procedures: (Describe simply in your own words what you will do and say.)

Day 1:

Day 2:

Day 3:

Day 4:

Use the Pedagogy and Procedures Checklist to describe specific activities for the students. Try to use as many of the various instructional procedures as possible for your four daily lessons. Refer to the checklist to remember options and check off when you use one by using a number from 1 to 4 to indicate which day you used the strategy. (If we are ever to escape from our comfort zone and implement the wide-ranging pedagogy called for in school renewal research, we must begin to experiment with the strategies on a regular basis.) Keep the checklist handy during the class. Many times a spontaneous opportunity will arise to use one of the approaches. When this happens, check off the appropriate box and write a note describing how the implementation worked. When writing the procedures, indicate which item on the checklist applies next to the appropriate activity. Whenever an activity or instruction in your narrative can be related to a virtue, place the appropriate virtue in parentheses next to the sentence. When you reflect on your class, note which strategies you did not use and try to use them in following classes.

7. Homework: Assign homework that will help ensure that the students understand the lesson, its relevance to their individual lives and the larger context of their lives and environment, and a problem-solving skill.

8. Closure and Assessment: It is good if there is time to do some of this after each daily lesson, but if doing it at the end of the unit is sufficient. Say how you will put closure to the lesson and how you will tie things together in a meaningful way. Refer to *respect* and *responsibility* in this section and how the students understand the relationship among the lesson, the virtues, and respect and responsibility. Refer to both the academic and the character subject. Describe how you will determine the extent to which students attained the objective. (See "Measuring Success," below, and chapter 4 for a more thorough look at assessments.)

9. State how many opportunities you took to teach character development. This is why we ask you to underline each notation that refers the content lesson to the character lesson. By doing this you will begin to get a sense of how many times character can come into play without disrupting the class. In fact, you will find a balance point where the right amount of character education will enhance learning the course subject.

10. Note how many times you actually used one of the strategies or objectives on the Pedagogy and Procedures Checklist. Doing this will help motivate you to continue seeking ways to use them. It also will help you note the ones you tend not to use so you can make adjustments accordingly.

11. Give follow-up activities such as projects, homework, and assignments that relate to both the academic and the character subject.

12. Reflect on the strengths and weaknesses of your plan and how you implement it. Include references to the specific class since weak spots might relate to the unique group of individuals and not the plan or its delivery.

Measuring Success

Evaluation and assessment often are viewed as nuisances in spite of the outcry for them. We believe that reliable, formative assessments are an important ally for the teacher and the student. Outcome assessments in character education can show that emphasizing virtues has a positive effect on all aspects, participants, and goals of education. This has proven to be a daunting task, but we feel there is light at the end of the tunnel. The assessment approach described in chapter 4 refers to a potpourri of assessment strategies to validate the success of our lesson plans and emphasizes that "the process is the outcome." These include school and classroom climate measures; behavioral observations during contrived group tasks; teacher, student, and parent anecdotes and journals; portfolios; introspective questions; and several other methodologies.

These various measurement tools take into consideration the following axioms:

1. Assessment measures must be related to the level of learning addressed. For example, if understanding is key, then assess the extent of comprehension. If identification is the objective, then assess identification. In choosing specific lesson plan objectives for the

virtues, also consider the grade level and how well your students understand various concepts. In considering grade-level appropriateness, there are many variables to consider, and we feel professional teachers are in the best position to decide. Although some character education researchers, like Chip Wood, suggest the following schedule, our experience is that you can teach any of the virtues at any grade level if the right variables are in place.[9] Still, recommendations like Wood's help us to remember to keep our objectives in line with the levels of understanding our students seem to have. He suggests:

- Focus primarily on generosity and respect in kindergarten.
- Focus mostly on respect and honesty in first and second grades.
- Focus on teamwork and fortitude in grades three through five.
- Emphasize courage development in all its forms for grades six through eight.
- Concentrate on humility, responsibility, and patience in grades nine through 12.

You may find it easier to focus on just one or on a few virtues at a time during a class. We think you should use as many as naturally emerge in the lesson. If you and the students always have the core virtues in mind, and if you use a variety of effective teaching strategies and goals with your content areas, you and the students will know when to involve virtues in your work together. The bottom line is that whenever there is a true chance to teach any of the core virtues to any child at any age, go for it.

2. Daily or weekly assessments should be coordinated with a longitudinal strategy. Immediate learning outcomes should build on themselves and reveal themselves in a collective manner. Don't expect too much too soon, but make sure you have concrete, interrelated goals to pursue throughout the year(s). A danger of assessing virtues is thinking that after a four-day lesson, students will embody the traits that were taught and behave in such a way as to show you they have internalized the virtue. Building character will take more time, more teachers, and more experience. Allow for a movement from awareness to knowing to understanding to belief to applying to becoming over time.

There is another assessment concept we want to introduce, called "2 + 2" by Dr. Dwight Allen of Old Dominion College of Education. This simple approach to assessment is an extension of authentic assessment rationales and has significant potential for formative evaluations. All it calls for is telling the person being assessed the two most important accomplishments (good things) he or she did, followed by the two most important things that could be improved. This approach largely removes the usual anxieties associated with assessment, including "stereotype threat."[10] (Stereotype threat exists when any minority group feels that the test will stereotype it as inferior. When this feeling is present, test scores are significantly lower.)

SAMPLE LESSON PLAN FORMAT #1

Title
Teacher's Name:
Academic Subject:
Character Subject:
Thematic Unit Title:
Grade Level:
Time Allowed: Day 1 ___ Day 2 ___ Day 3 ___ Day 4 ___

Opening Questions
Academic:
Character:

Official Content Standard Addressed

Student Prerequisite Skills and Knowledge
Academic:
Character:

Resources and Materials

Learning Goals
Academic:
Character:

Specific Objectives
Academic:
Character:

Instructional Procedures

Number of Opportunities for Teaching Character Development

Number of Teaching Strategies Checked on Pedagogy and Procedures Checklist

Strategies on Checklist Not Used

Homework

Closure and Assessment

Follow-up Activities and Homework

Personal Reflection

Note: You may use this form, use the block form on the next two pages (as we do for the sample plans in subsequent chapters), or create your own format.

SAMPLE LESSON PLAN FORMAT #2

Title	Learning Goals	Official Content Standard Addressed
• Academic subject: • Character subject: • Grade level: • Time allowed: • Date last modified:	Academic: Character:	

Specific Objectives		Resources and Materials
Academic: Character:		

Student Prerequisite Skills/Knowledge	Opening Questions	
Academic: Character:	Academic: Character:	

Instructional Procedures

Number of Opportunities for Teaching Character Development

Number of Strategies Checked on Pedagogical Checklist

Strategies on Checklist Not Used

Closure and Assessment

Follow-up Activities and Homework

Personal Reflection

Questions for Student Teachers

1. Referring to the conceptual model, describe the interactions and cycles it conveys.
2. List as many virtues as you and your class can think of and see if and how they might be related to the six core universal virtues listed in the conceptual model.
3. Use the following chapter to help you define all the terms used in the conceptual model.
4. What does it mean to have "intentionality" for teaching virtues?
5. Why is it that opportunities for embedding virtues into a class lesson are more likely to emerge if a variety of teaching strategies on the Pedagogy and Procedures Checklist are used?
6. Describe the difference between inculcating virtues and cultivating virtues in your students.

Notes

1. Recall the definition of spirituality offered in the introduction as being a concern for the great questions about existence rather than answers to these questions. The concern comes from the realization of our interconnectedness. Perhaps this understanding is what American Indian cultures have to offer our current civilization. In spite of the hundreds of unique cultures, all Indian spiritual practices had in common respect for all of life and gratitude toward a great spirit for having provided it. Contrast this with cultures that have murdered and tortured people who did not believe in a particular religion and who continue to disagree among themselves about spiritual matters.

2. The call for an "across the curriculum" approach to character education comes from the Character Education Partnership, Boston University's Center for the Advancement of Ethics, and University of San Diego's International Center for Character Education.

3. There is a growing body of research that shows how character education, when it includes certain prerequisites, can achieve the desired results in both character building and academics. See De-Roche and Williams (1998). The key ingredient for success is teaching virtues across the curriculum. This occurs in some of the basic school models that follow Ernest Boyer's ideas (Boyer, 1995), such as Irving B. Weber's elementary school in Iowa City, Iowa, directed by its principal, Dr. Celia R. Burger.

However, most of the character education programs implemented in schools around the country do not meet the "across the curriculum" or consistency requirement. They offer thematic units sporadically, have one period or course a week or each month devoted to character development, or merely post character reminders on walls. This problem occurs even with programs that agree with the need to implement an across the curriculum approach.

4. Whenever you come across a word like *holistic* we suggest you look it up in chapter 3 so we can be sure to build on words and ideas with consistent understanding.

5. Kohl, 1984, p. 14.

6. In his book, *Educating for an Ecologically Sustainable Culture: Rethinking Moral Education, Creativity, Intelligence and Other Modern Orthodoxies*, C. A. Bowers shows how we cannot have an ecologically sustainable culture when our educational institutions continue to reinforce the very aspects of culture that are devastating the environment.

7. These four requirements for effective character education come from the excellent research published in *Integrated Character Education* edited by Timothy Rusnak, 1998.

8. We have selected Howard Gardner's multiple intelligences for our checklist because each domain brings up new opportunities to evoke or discuss the virtues. When used with our spiritual and nature orientation, such diverse focuses can enhance character development. However, a danger of latching blindly onto the multiple intelligence framework is allowing it to support an overly indi-

vidualistic and anthropocentric view of reality. When this happens, a relativistic worldview (where virtues are seen as relative to situations or cultures) emerges to support consumerism and ignore our dependence on ecological systems. For example, a musical orientation in American Indian culture is a way to develop and perpetuate a process of life-enhancing relationships. Too often, we use the multiple intelligences strictly as a way to elicit individualistic aptitudes without regard to the cultural and natural systems that surround the individual's life. For a thorough discussion of this potential problem, see Bowers' *Educating for an Ecologically Sustainable Culture*.

9. Wood, 1999, p. 299.

10. Work conducted by Dr. Claude M. Steele of Stanford University indicates that whenever a minority group perceives that a test might confirm a stereotype against that group, a self-fulfilling prophecy emerges. (See his article, "Thin Ice," published in the August 1999 issue of *Atlantic Monthly*, vol. 284, no. 7, pp. 44–54.)

Chapter 3

Words and Meanings

Truth is an eternal conversation about things that matter,
conducted with passion and discipline.
— Parker Palmer, *The Courage to Teach*

It doesn't interest me if the story you're telling me is true.
I want to know if you can disappoint another to be true to yourself;
if you can bear betrayal and not betray your own soul.
I want to know if you can be faithful and therefore trustworthy.
— Oriah Mountain Dreamer, *Dreams of Desire*

The word good has many meanings. For example, if a man
were to shoot his grandmother at a range of 500 yards,
I should call him a good shot, but not necessarily a good man.
— G. K. Chesterton, "Negative and Positive Morality," *Illustrated London News*

Now that we have introduced our conceptual model and pedagogical checklist, it is important to clarify some of the terms and phrases we use in them. When referring to the virtues, teaching strategies, or concepts, it may be helpful for you to have a sense of our meanings and your own definitions in mind before writing your new lesson plans or modifying your old ones.

The Futility of Another's Wisdom

Don's Story

I once wrote an article about living life to the fullest and expressing one's positive mental, physical, creative, social, and spiritual potential. A friend, both a wise man and an esteemed colleague of mine, reviewed it and told me I should throw it away.

"Why?" I asked. Was it that bad?"

His answer disturbed me for years. He told me it was not bad at all. In fact, he said it was "right on target." He said it explained exactly the problems and the solutions for unhappy people and corrupt societies, but that "it doesn't leave me or anyone else any place to go on our own." His remarks were final, and he gestured that he had no more to say on the subject.

It took me years to really understand what my colleague meant. Over that time I found that my passion and my ability to use words to convey important ideas often encountered a kind of hostility or resentment in some of my students. Eventually, I came to realize my problem. Wisdom is a wonderful goal, but each of us must find it on our own. Those of us compelled to share what wisdom we have learned on our unique paths risk alienating those who are not ready to move in the direction of our own interest or focus. This is a great challenge for teachers.

So why do we teach, write, inspire, encourage, and hope our words can make a difference? I suggest the answer rests with the metaphor of planting seeds that may take hold in time—in our students' own time. If our ideas are sound and useful, our students will benefit from them when they are ready to tie them into their own world of experience.

Jessica's Story

I don't know if I agree with the seed planting metaphor exactly. I prefer a road map metaphor. When traveling into a new area we all benefit from a good road map or, if hiking, a good trail map. With it, we tend to go in the right direction with a bit more security and less wasted time than without the map. The journey is still ours, however. In fact, if someone takes us everywhere, we lose much of what we might have learned on our own.

I had a student in my math class who just did not get the formulas and the methods for solving a particular geometry problem, no matter how hard I tried. One day for a test I told the class that I did not care how they got to an answer or even if the answer was the same one on my answer sheet. I just wanted to see them work through the material to learn how they were thinking about math.

Well, the student having so much trouble amazed me! He came up with the right answers to a variety of problems, but he used an approach I had never seen before. I think this story makes the same point about giving people room to learn on their own.

No Final Words

We preface these definitions with the above stories because we know our choices and our definitions are not the only options, nor are they the final words on the subject. We do not expect anyone to incorporate our approach or interpret our ideas exactly as we suggest and we hope you will give the same latitude to your students.

We also are aware that terms like *respect* or *responsibility* can be used to lead students toward mere obedience to authority. In his book, *Schools without Failure*, William Glasser observed that many teachers "teach thoughtless conformity to school rules and call the conforming child 'responsible.'"[1] The exhortation to "be respectful to adults" might mean something entirely different from that which might lead to good character. Therefore, when reading our definitions and writing your own for the words below, keep in mind our goal to use understanding of these concepts and virtues as a way to create self-actualized, caring individuals, who will live in ways that demonstrate an awareness that "we are all related."

Definitions

Respect: In American Indian traditional cultures, arbitrary, external, or institutionalized authority that allows people to control others has no legitimacy. Respect is not demanded by or given to such authority figures. Rather, respect is an inherent recognition of deeply felt relatedness to others. It is about understanding that everyone and everything has a role to play in the web of life and deserves at least our sincere attention. We recommend using this idea to guide your discussions and definitions regarding the concept of "respect."

Your definition of respect:

Responsibility: We see this term as the action associated with the feeling respect engenders in us. It relates to the accountability and reciprocity called for by the very nature of being related. Being responsible requires practicing the virtues that lead to good character whenever an obligation to respect for our interrelatedness emerges.

Your definition of responsibility:

Good Character: A person with good character consistently lives according to and strongly identifies with a firm code of ethics and virtues, recognizes and cherishes the interconnections of all creatures, and lives with a high degree of peacefulness in his or her heart. We understand that this is an evolving process.

Your definition of good character:

Character Education: This refers to a teaching and learning system that emphasizes the development of universally recognized virtues such as courage, generosity, respectfulness, fortitude, and honesty. It assumes that good thoughts and behaviors must come before smart thoughts and behaviors. It embraces a variety of proven approaches to teaching and learning that are necessary for helping students to internalize these virtues.

Your definition of character education:

Virtue: Like many character educators, we make the important distinction between "values" and "virtues." Values clarification and religious training have a place in the development of character, but both can be obstacles to development when such values become competitive or ignore another's values. Virtues make the world a better place for all. Values are what are important to you; they may or may not make the world a better place. The distinction is important if we are to break through the barriers that stand in the way of widespread character education, especially the standard, "Whose values anyway?" question.

One day the faculty at Oglala Lakota College asked a group of education majors to come to a consensus on six of the most important traits that define a good person or a person with "good character." Although the usual, universal choices such as courage, fortitude, patience, humility, truthfulness and generosity, came up in the discussion, others insisted that culture or the Lakota language was most important. There was even some resentment that we asserted that these virtues were "universal" and that people from all cultures tend to list them when given the same assignment.

It is true that Indian languages have encoded ways of thinking that emphasize good character. However, our natural relationships with nature and each other are now in conflict with more materialistic interactions. Speaking the language is no longer sufficient in and of itself (though every effort to keep the language alive will help communicate the old ways). If we do not teach and give priority to the virtues through experiences and integrated curriculum, it will not be enough to practice ceremonies or use languages originally intended to coincide with such teaching. Cultural richness without conscious attention to the stories that teach character will not bring back our health, wisdom, and sovereignty if we do not emphasize the virtues *first*, and then emphasize the useful parts of the culture that support the virtues, leaving the less useful parts behind.

It is common for values that relate to one's identity, specific knowledge, power, or even freedom to be confused with the virtues. Knowledge, power, group affiliations, or the goal of freedom do not consistently cause us to make good moral choices in our lives. Courage, generosity, patience and fortitude do. Values may be extremely important, even vital, but values without virtues can be a menace.

Your definition of virtue:

The Six Virtues

The six "core universal virtues" that we have selected for our model are on every list of the important virtues we have seen. We have selected these six also because we believe that, in concert with the other dimensions of our conceptual model, they are basic to the many others. For example, being appreciative is a virtue, but it calls for generosity of heart and spirit. To truly give of one's self allows for being sincerely thankful. Prayerfulness is a virtue, but when we recognize our interconnectedness to all in the seen and unseen realms, how can we not be prayerful?

In any event, feel free to choose any core virtues to use in your work. In fact, we recommend that your class come to a consensus regarding four to six virtues that you can focus on throughout the year. Careful discussions ultimately conclude that the balance that our six provide when used in light of respect, responsibility, wisdom, and spirituality makes them ideal. The Council for Global Education lists the following traits: assertiveness, caring compassion, confidence, consideration, courage, courtesy, detachment, determination, forgiveness, friendliness, generosity, gentleness, helpfulness, honesty, humility, justice, kindness, love, loyalty, mercy, patience, prayerfulness, respect, reverence, self-discipline, service, steadfastness, tact, thankfulness, tolerance, trust, trustworthiness, truthfulness, and unity.[2]

You may also want to choose virtues that cannot be described with just one word. For example, in the Lakota language there is a word, *tehinda*, which translates to a genuine feeling or honoring of children and a treasuring of life. Another is "He is *iyepi* which means it's his life, let him choose, do not be judgmental. If your students conclude that such concepts are universal virtues (as opposed to local values), then they might be added to your list of definitions.

We have noticed that many of the texts on character do not attempt to define the virtues that relate to being a person of good character. They seem to assume that we all have a good understanding of what we mean when we say *courage* or *patience,* but our experience is that many people benefit from a little refresher on these concepts. Remember, our descriptions of the terms are not the final word. In fact, we ask that after reading our definition, you write your own in the space provided (and give your students a similar opportunity to use their own words to define the terms). In the final analysis, we all touch some universal understanding of the great virtues, but, ultimately, our unique differences keep anyone from claiming a perfect definition for everyone. This allows a certain mystery to surround the virtues, and this is good.

Fortitude: This is about sticking with something that is worthwhile. It relates to enduring until the goal is reached. Fortitude requires the willingness to suffer some, if necessary, to do what is right, good, or healthful over the long haul. When people have this character trait, they do not take the easy way out or emphasize convenience to overshadow these things.

Your definition of fortitude:

Courage: Courage or bravery was defined by Lakota educator Pat Locke as the "strength of character which equips us to meet danger and trouble, to live our values, and to tell the truth in the face of ignorance."[3] We cannot think of a better definition. Courage is the quality of mind that enables us to risk what we value for a higher purpose.

Your definition of courage:

Patience: Like all great things, the virtues blend into one another. They are interconnected. Patience, courage, and fortitude especially share common requirements. Patience, as we see it however, does not relate as much to fear of risking something, as courage does. Nor does it relate as much to enduring through action as fortitude does. Patience is more about waiting, tolerating, and forgiving. We are patient when we give others their own space and time. People who are patient are not easily provoked or vengeful, and they tend to remain calm during stressful situations.

Your definition of patience:

Honesty: An honest person, in our opinion, does what he or she says. Honesty is about being trustworthy. People with this character trait truly care about truth, and here we want to repeat Parker Palmer's definition of truth: "conversation about things that matter conducted with passion and discipline." The passion is about sincerity, and the discipline relates to the five inner skills in the conceptual model. We see honesty as a subcategory of integrity.

Your definition of honesty:

Humility: American Indian people generally feel that many non-Indian people misunderstand this virtue. We regard humility as the essential ingredient for learning with all of our senses. We can listen and pay true attention to something only when we let go of our preconceptions. We cannot feel any arrogance toward nature and its creatures. We cannot assume we already know the answers or that we are better or higher than another. To us, humility is not about humiliation, self-abasement, penitence for sin, or being unworthy in the sight of God. Humility, as we define it, is freedom from pride and arrogance that recognizes equity and equality. It is manifested by a great appreciation for the many gifts life and God have to offer us. One of the best ways to experience humility is amidst the grandeur of the natural world.

Your definition of humility:

Generosity: Generosity is one of the most apparent virtues among American Indians. Lakota people actually measure their worth by how much they give away. Those not influenced greatly by western culture's emphasis on material wealth still do. Generosity is about giving and/or sharing our time, our wealth, our ideas, or our possessions in behalf of others. One way to think of it is as the opposite of greed or selfishness. A person with this trait balances well taking care of self and taking care of others.

Your definition of generosity:

Spirituality: Spirituality refers to a genuine awareness of our great and mysterious connections with all aspects of the universe, both seen and unseen, and it includes the realization that there is a sacred force behind these interconnections. Spirituality is more about the concern for great questions regarding life and death than about specific answers, which is the realm of the great religions. In American Indian thinking about spirituality, the great mystery about life is part of what makes it sacred. This kind of thinking honors all religions but cannot understand why people have been tortured or murdered if they do not choose one or the other. It allows us to consider that trees and animals may have souls and deserve respect.[4] Once we begin to pick and choose who or what has value, the great virtues detour from respect and wisdom, and then even courage, patience, and fortitude can be used for destructive purposes.

Ecological awareness is a vital aspect of spirituality. If we are indeed a part of a vast, mysterious, and complex web of life, how can we continue to ignore what we are doing to our natural environment and the many life forms that surround us? Good character education keeps in mind the issues of sustainability, interdependence, diversity, and partnerships and acknowledges the wonderful mystery of life in which we are all entwined.

Love, compassion, and caring also flows out of true spiritual awareness. If we see everything as related to us, and if we view these relationships as sacred, these three emotions are unavoidable.

Your definition of spirituality:

Integrity: We use integrity to describe what one has when one firmly adheres to and identifies with virtues for the right reasons and when no one is looking. Integrity is acting on the awareness of spirituality. The origin of the word, *integer*, is about *oneness*. Integrity is a synonym for *good character*, except that good character also, by our definition, calls for the following trait (peacefulness).

Your definition of integrity:

Peacefulness: Note that in the conceptual model *good character* means high degrees of integrity and peacefulness. The word we use in the Lakota language for this idea is *wolakota*. Either refers to a sense of peacefulness in *all relations*. Rigid adherence to a code of behavior without this sense of peacefulness can be militaristic, sanctimonious, or, at best, exhausting. Albert Schweitzer conveyed the importance of calmness on the road to character when he said, "Anyone who proposes to do good must not expect people to roll stones out of his way, but must accept his lot calmly, even if they roll a few stones upon it." Without this sense of peacefulness, frustration with barriers to character education easily can cause us to violate the principles and virtues we have learned to cherish. It is difficult to teach peacefulness without using some form of meditation. Even with such moments of quiet receptivity, peacefulness is usually something that comes from living a life that is guided by spiritual awareness of the invisible realms of existence.

Your definition of peacefulness:

The Five Inner Skills

Reason: Without reason, the ways of learning, life experience, and training in virtues cannot be internalized sufficiently to develop good character or to be consistent with virtuous living. Reason is the function of the mind that develops and grows in the light of experience, learning strategies, and virtues. And, when it is working well, it is also the judge of these things.

Logic is a part of reason, as are knowledge and information. Reasoning is a tricky business, however, and only leads to wisdom when its conclusions have been applied sufficiently in life's experience.

Your definition of reason:

Intuition: Relying too much on reason has gotten us into trouble. Reason uses a foundation of personal history, interpretations of self and others, and information that may not be true. Scientific facts that lead us to reasonable conclusions in one decade may make no sense at all in the next. This is because humans cannot know all of the mysteries of reality, even if we think we can. Intuition is the skill of the mind to tap into truth without regard to reason. Intuition is often thought of as unconscious memories. However, we prefer to think of it as an ability to tune in to the vibrations of the universal consciousness or, if you will, to the voice of the Great Spirit.

Your definition of intuition:

Reflection: We use reflection to refer to the use of both reason and intuition when assessing or evaluating experience. But it goes beyond mere evaluation. It considers alternatives and asks if actions are for the greatest good of all. Reflection helps make us responsible. It gives us wisdom for continual improvement.

Your definition of reflection:

Humor: Another wonderful lesson we can all learn from Indian country is about humor, a characteristic most noticeable in medicine men and women. Indian people are very quick to laugh, in spite of the harshest environments or situations. Tom Allen says that real humor is seeing the disjunction of things.[5] Humor understands that there is a bigger picture behind the scenes. It is recognizing the frailties we all share, whatever our position in life. If you are sure to include humor in your lesson plans, it will be easier to convey ideas about the great virtues. Humor can foster courage, fortitude, and humility as much as any other phenomenon.

Your definition of humor:

Emotional management: In his book, *Emotional Intelligence*, Daniel Goleman says that we cannot evaluate or make choices that are congruent with our virtues or reasoning powers if we are not aware of our emotional reactions and if we are unable to control them.[6] This does not mean that reason, intuition, courage, patience, humor, recreation, or any of the other terms in our conceptual model graph do not influence emotional control. It simply means we must be aware of our emotions and how they influence us. Recalling the CAT-FAWN connection, this includes remembering why we have emotional reactions in the first place.

Your definition of emotional management:

The External Skills

Mastery of survival: We believe strongly that survival is every bit or more about virtues than about knowledge, not only for personal survival, but also for survival of our species. However, we intend this category to focus more on the external skills that apply reading, writing, basic math, and effective communication to appropriate, age-relevant survival situations. For example, lesson plans for math should solve real problems. Reading lessons might involve grocery shopping and ingredient lists. Speaking skills that show a young child how to ask for assistance or how to call 911 are also be a way to teach mastery of survival.

Ultimately, we think that teaching survival skills is about relevancy to our students' needs and interests. Unfortunately, this is often missing in education. A wonderful letter from Indian leaders of the Six Nations illustrates how obvious this was to American Indians from the beginning of associations with white man's education. On June 17, 1744, commissioners from Maryland and Virginia negotiated a treaty with the Six Nations people at Lancaster, Pennsylvania. The Indians were invited to send boys to William and Mary College, but the next day they declined the offer with this letter:

> We know that you highly esteem the kind of learning taught in those colleges, and that the maintenance of our young men, while with you, would be very expensive to you. We are convinced that you mean to do us good by your proposal; and we thank you heartily. But you, who are wise must know that different nations have different conceptions of things and you will therefore not take it amiss if our ideas of this kind of education happen not to be the same as yours. We have had some experience of it. Several of our young people were formerly brought up at the colleges of the northern provinces: they were instructed in all your sciences; but, when they came back to us, they were bad runners, ignorant of every means of living in the woods . . . neither fit for hunters warriors, nor counselors, they were totally good for nothing.
>
> We are, however, not the less oblig'd by your kind offer, tho' we decline accepting it; and, to show our grateful sense of it, if the gentlemen of Virginia will send us a dozen of their sons, we will take care of their education, instruct them in all we know, and make men of them.[7]

Occupational mastery: How much emphasis you place on occupational mastery in your lesson plans depends, of course, on the grade level. For most children, however, some level of relevance between the subject matter and its usefulness in getting (and keeping) a job seems important to us. Although we think it is unfortunate that so many policy makers believe that the primary goal of education is for the United States to be more competitive in the global marketplace, we hope that people who graduate from high school and/or college have skills they can use to earn a decent living. Tying subject matter content standards to specific kinds of jobs helps motivate students and improves understanding of the connections we hope we are making.

Character education is an important factor in occupational mastery, as well. In fact, ethics is a hot topic in most corporations today. The U.S. Naval Academy just started a mandatory course in Integrity Development for all of its students. Students can begin learning early on about the relationship between the virtues and being a good, happy, and successful employee or employer. It might help us all if they also realized the value of ethics in making business decisions that could have negative affects on other people or the environment.

Recreational mastery: We all know the adage about all work and no play. It seems too many of us have forgotten how to recreate. Our vacations are usually two weeks of escape to some expensive paradise we cannot afford. Here is perhaps another area where our Indian brothers' and sisters' ancient philosophy can help us out. Participation in games, music, and art are interwoven into the fabric of American Indian life. We should underline the word, *participation.* Too many of our children grow up thinking that recreation is only something we watch on television or in a football stadium. Many wind up as adults who avoid anything that smacks of personal competition because they have bad memories of an exaggerated emphasis on winning and losing. As a result, people are reluctant to try new skills for fear of injuring their egos. Whenever possible, our lesson plans should encourage participation. They should emphasize another adage that has only been given lip service of late: It is not whether you win or lost, but how you play the game.

Pedagogy and Procedures Checklist Terms

1. **Cooperative learning:** This describes any activity in which students collaborate with one or more people in the learning process. This includes working with parents, community members, or other students. It describes a mutually beneficial relationship between people where responsibility, authority, and accountability for learning are shared.

2. **Field experience:** Check this item in your lesson plan if your students leave the classroom to learn or apply knowledge in real-life situations. How do field trips increase natural opportunities for teaching character? Think about taking your class of fourth graders into the South Dakota badlands to look for fossils or to the Smithsonian Institution. Now imagine how the six virtues and the inner and outer skills can be addressed. Remember, we are not referring to those times when students blatantly disregard virtues. Teaching virtues when children are misbehaving is not ideal because children not only are paying too little attention, but they actually may rebel against the concept in the throes of anger.

3. **Intrinsic motivational strategy:** Is there anything in your lesson plans that you intend as a way to trigger self-motivation in your students? In *Education on the Edge of Possibility*, Renate and Geoffrey Caine write, "Deep meanings are the source of most intrinsic motivation."[8] Anything you do that truly gives your students an opportunity to reflect on how the lesson relates to them will allow you to put a check by this strategy.

4. **Extrinsic motivational strategy:** Carrot and stick approaches to motivation are overused in most classrooms. Their effect in the learning process is too often temporary and can create a materialistic mindset and a loss of personal initiative to do good or to learn deeply. However, when used carefully and judiciously, well-thought-out rewards and consequences that are logical for the situation can be useful.

5. **Student ownership of subject matter:** Did you involve the students in helping determine what aspects of the subject are most important, or in what ways it could best be learned? Anything you say, ask, or do that helps to give the students ownership meets the requirements for this pedagogy.

6. **Critical thinking exercises:** If your assignments, directions, encouragements, or questions are intended to stimulate critical questions and thoughts about the subject, about your presentation of the subject, or about the learning process related to the subject, then you are using this approach to learning. Critical pedagogy does not give absolute answers, but rather asks questions such as: What do you think about it? It teaches young people to be informed consumers of information in the same way our Reddie Rabbit character taught children about Saturday morning television commercials and cigarette advertisements.

   Critical thinking is an important and, too often, missing aspect of teaching and learning. Here again, Indian people serve as a model. Indians judge truth in relation to experience, reason, intuition, and the wisdom inherent in nature, and, even then, they remain willing to accept a degree of uncertainty. This is a far cry from the tendency to perceive reality based exclusively on the words of a human authority figure.[9]

7. **Intuitive exercises:** Remember that character education relates to the spiritual awareness of visible and invisible connections. By offering opportunities for your students to experiment with their intuitions, they learn to trust the existence of this invisible world. Intuition can tap unconscious knowledge. Such intuitive information has two sources: the first is unconscious memories from previous experiences, and the second is the one most important to indigenous people—expression of an awareness of universal knowledge. Having students guess something about the subject by tuning in to it is an example of an intuitive exercise.

8. **Visualizations:** The use of guided visualizations with students is, unfortunately, controversial. We say unfortunate because you are very unlikely to do any harm by offering positive suggestions while someone is using his or her imagination to perceive a situation, feeling, or information. In fact, it is a tragedy that visualization strategies that use such hypnotic learning are used so rarely in the classroom. A world-class athlete would not think of learning to improve his or her athletic skills without such inner-mind strategies. Although you might ask a student to imagine something that could bring up bad memo-

ries, if you are aware of your students during visualization exercises, it is easy to bring the student back to the present time and place with confident, pleasant words. Teachers' words do far more damage to unconscious minds throughout the course of a normal day when teachers are unaware of the image-producing quality of what they say.[10] Asking students to relax, close their eyes, and imagine being in a place that might help them better understand the subject matter is indeed an effective strategy for learning.

9. **Dramatizations:** Human beings need drama in their lives. Drama keeps us in balance by giving an outlet to our negative energies. It is a dimension of story telling in which the students themselves are the characters. If you use a dramatization to illustrate a lesson or to help your students learn a subject, check this number in your lesson plan.

10. **Emotional management opportunity:** Too often we forget the idea of prevention as teachers and therefore have to resort to postvention when it comes to inappropriate behaviors relating to emotional loss of control in our students. Giving students of all ages opportunities to control their emotions through role-playing, discussions, and real-life situations before problems arise is a vital aspect of character education.

The Orientations

In addition to our spiritual orientation, implicit in all of our teaching goals, we list eight *orientations*. Although the first seven of these originate with Howard Gardner's work, good educators have always known that different people tend to excel in these different areas. Using one orientation gives students a chance to experience an intelligence with which they are less unfamiliar. It also gives those who have that particular intelligence a chance to excel where they may be weak in traditional logical thinking.

We believe that if you use a variety of these orientations, they will expose new ways to relate virtues to everyday living quite naturally. We do not see these orientations in terms of individual intelligences so much as we see them as different ways of accessing and expressing relatedness. So we ask that care be taken to maintain a balance between the typically individualistic, autonomous approach to these orientations and our more holistic, community-based approach.

11. **Musical orientation:** The musical orientation is a very important one, and it is losing ground in our schools. We can learn much from the American Indian perspective on this vital phenomenon. Indians all participate in singing; it is not relegated to the very talented or specially trained individuals only. Every task and every event has a song to describe and celebrate it. Songs record and remind us of our histories. In nearly every Indian myth, the creator sings things into life. Therefore, Indians recognize the power of musical vibrations.

    Whether you play background music, or use rhythm, singing, or any other aspect of music to teach a lesson, note on your checklist and in your lesson plan that you used this approach.

12. **Logical orientation:** When our lesson plans, curriculum, and pedagogy deal with inductive and deductive thinking, numbers or scientific methodology, we are using a logical orientation.

13. **Spatial orientation:** Students use this orientation when they imagine, visualize, or sense ideas in their mind's eye. In a world that exaggerates logical orientation and relegates mental imagery to only younger youth, we lose this vital skill. We place art in this orientation in all of its forms, as well. Of course, some people are naturally stronger in this area than others, but it is a muscle that is best exercised by everyone if we are to walk in harmony. Many logical conclusions do little good until they are internalized through some form of spatial orientation.

14. **Linguistic orientation:** We have talked about the power of words, especially during various states of concentration. Activities or lessons that relate to written and spoken language describe this orientation.

15. **Kinesthetic orientation:** When your lessons involve motor activities, dance, physical movement, balancing, and/or coordination as part of the learning process, such as playing catch while doing multiplication tables, then the kinesthetic orientation is being exercised, and those especially gifted in this area tend to learn better during such activities.

16. **Interpersonal orientation:** This is the orientation that comes into play during cooperating or team learning. It has to do with person-to-person relationships and communication. It also calls for emotional control, generosity, and other important virtues and skills.

17. **Intrapersonal orientation:** Besides learning to have healthy relationships with others, walking the road to good character requires that we have a healthy relationship with ourselves. Opportunities for self-reflection, as when using the CAT-FAWN connection, call on this orientation. Creative writing about personal experiences or activities that do not involve others may also employ this particular intelligence. Giving students intrapersonal exercises can foster an appreciation for the six virtues as they learn to know themselves, where they are, and what they need to learn about the virtues.

18. **Nature orientation:** We already talked about the importance of remembering our true relationship to nature when we introduced American Indian perspectives as they related to CAT-FAWN. It is no less important that we think of ways to get our kids involved with nature while in school. Our sample lesson plans illustrate this, but we strongly recommend Michael Cohen's book, *Connecting with Nature*.[11] It has simple exercises that students can do, even in the inner city, that take advantage of our natural affinity for nature in the learning process. No degree of personal development of any kind amounts to much if we allow our children to inherit a world in which we can neither breathe clean air nor drink clean water.

19. **Community involvement:** This relates to any opportunities in your lesson plans for involving the community outside the classroom. This could mean the surrounding community or a group of people in another state or country. Such activities make learning more meaningful because they illustrate our interconnectedness with our community members and those of other communities.

20. **Multicultural aspects:** It is not difficult to include study, or even acknowledgement, other cultures when designing a lesson plan in any of the content areas. By so doing, we cultivate recognition and respect for the similarities and differences of other cultures and teach our students that all cultures have something to contribute to making the world a better place. Diversity is a key to success in the future, but it must be honored now.

21. **Service-learning activity:** A service-learning experience differs from community involvement above in that this is an opportunity for students to help or serve others in a community. Service learning is about genuinely giving of oneself to help another or the environment. For service learning to be effective in character building, it must have three ingredients. First, students should understand the reasons for the particular service before they offer their assistance, and these reasons should go beyond self-improvement objectives, focusing rather on genuine service to community. Second, they should experience the planning and effort required in accomplish the task at hand. Third, they should reflect on and discuss the project afterward to capture what was truly learned.

    This last requirement is crucial for character development and deserves a story to illustrate its importance. A teenage boy named Ben with a history of violence was incarcerated in a residential treatment center. He continued to bully everyone around him, even at the center. His teacher asked him if he would like to join the choir that was planning to sing at a nearby senior citizen's home. The boy laughingly agreed, and it was obvious he only did so to get off-campus.

    Ben endured several weeks of rehearsals, learning songs from the 1940s. When the time came to sing for the old folks, he reluctantly joined in with the others. Afterward, the teacher sat down with everyone and began the reflection and dialogue part of the service-learning experience. When the teacher asked Ben what he thought about what they had done, Ben laughed and said the whole thing was a joke. He referred to one of the seniors and said the old man did not even hear the singing! On hearing this comment, one of Ben's few friends spoke up. He explained that the old man Ben referred to did look like he was about to die and grabbed him as they were leaving, nearly scaring him to death. The boy said the old man pulled him down and whispered in his ear that the singing brought back wonderful memories of his long-departed wife.

    Ben listened to his friend and tears came to his eyes. Ben stopped bullying from that point on and became a role model at the school. Two years after his discharge, he was still doing fine.

22. **Interdisciplinary connection:** One problem with most school subjects is that they are separated from other, closely related subjects. Character education opportunities are more likely to arise when students really see the connections among things. By combining science with language arts or math with physical education, you give real examples of these connections. Whenever your lesson plans or thematic units integrate different subjects, check this number on the Pedagogy and Procedures Checklist.

23. **Dialogue opportunity:** Too often teaching is a one-way phenomenon. In his book, *The Courage to Teach*, Parker Palmer says, "Truth is a dialogue about things that matter conducted with passion and discipline." Dialogue about a subject affords many openings for interjecting ideas about universal virtues. If you plan on using dialogue in your lesson(s), check this one.

24. **Use of technology:** Technology is an essential tool for anyone's future. It may also present some opportunities for learning about character education programs and components. If computer research on some subject is tied to virtues, however, then it is not a far stretch to consider technology as a vehicle for teachable moments for character education.

    Owing to the emphasis on technology, we offer some words of caution. Our overdependence on science and technology has increased our expectation that our social problems can be solved through technology. It is a false expectation in many ways. Portland State University education Professor C. A. Bowers argues that our culture's emphasis on technology is sacrificing the "subtle, contextual and memory-based knowledge gleaned from living in a nature-based society and nourished by interactive learning with other humans and an ecologically based value system."[12] Similarly, the authors of *The Social Life of Information* say that distance education is an oxymoron.[13] Personally, we think that character education priority is way too far behind technology priority. Until it catches up, technology is likely to make character development even more difficult.

    On the other hand, when used intentionally as a way to build character in school, technology can be valuable. It opens up new worlds and new contacts with which to communicate and discuss ideas about social reform and healthy relationships. There is also enough material on the Web about character education to give any student or teacher a wealth of information about it.

25. **Use of humor:** Recall that humor is one of the inner skills depicted on our Conceptual Model. Without humor in the learning environment, we lose our connections with one another and began to take our ignorance about so many things too seriously. In a sense, we lose our spirit. We stop trusting in others until we lose faith in something greater than any of the lessons that keep us on task in spite of our frustrations.

    It is like the mountain climber who slipped at the top of a 10,000-foot peak and tumbled faster and faster down the slope toward a sheer dropoff. Just before he reached the edge, he managed to grab hold of a tree limb. Hanging there, thousands of feet above the ground, he screamed, "Helllllp! Help. Can anyone hear me?!"

    Suddenly a deep voice echoed through the air. "Yes. I am here," it said.

    "God, God is that you?" the climber asked.

    "It is," the voice answered solemnly.

    "Oh God, thank you. What do you want me to do?" the climber pleaded.

    "Do you have faith my son?" the voice resonated.

    "Yes, God," said the climber.

    "Then let go of the branch," God spoke with authority.

    "Hellllp. Is there anyone *else* up there?" cried the climber.

Even if we can't remember jokes, we can keep a sense of humor and encourage healthy, caring humor and laughing in our classrooms. If you do not do this, both you and your students are likely to lose faith in the learning process. When this happens, we lose the joy.

26. **Reference to wellness/fitness:** Next to character or moral development, wellness and fitness issues are the most undervalued priorities in education today. A third of our elementary school children are overweight. Heart disease and diabetes are making inroads on teenagers. In Indian country we are especially concerned about this. Here, the use of nontraditional foods, cigarettes, and alcohol are killing people in epidemic proportions. Indians were once noted for their endurance, but as a result of being forced into the priorities, lifestyles, and negative habits of the dominant culture, many have become horribly ill. This example might be the greatest lesson we can learn from Indian people.

    In schools around the country, soft drink and candy machines are convenient. Regular, aerobic exercise for health, as opposed to competition, is becoming rare. We could go on and on of course. (Recall our book, *Happy Exercise*, that we wrote years ago as a partial solution to this problem.) Our point here is that neither we nor our students are going to be able to walk the talk of the great virtues without the confidence, emotional strength, and physical and mental endurance that can come only from a fit body. We hope that, somehow, a little learning or motivation about this subject, even in the math class, can help tie fitness and wellness concepts into our overall game plan.

27. **Opportunities for learning via peer teaching:** In essence, peer teaching has similar benefits as service learning and, in fact, peer teaching is an excellent service-learning activity. In this category we mean for students to learn in the way research shows we all learn best—by teaching what it is we want to learn. (This is why teaching virtues may help all teachers become more virtuous.)

28. **Mediation:** Training in conflict resolution skills can be useful for children as young as kindergarten age. Such training has the best results when people are getting along. Too often we wait until conflicts occur to attempt to teach mediation. By incorporating mediation awareness or skills in lesson plans across the curriculum, many natural opportunities for character education will emerge.

29. **Story-telling:** Many people are aware of the value placed on story-telling in American Indian cultures. One reason story-telling is such a wonderful teaching mechanism is that it gives each listener a chance to gain his or her own lesson from the story. Story-telling uses several of the multiple intelligences. Humor and drama are often involved, which, as we have discussed, are vital for human learning and health. The stories of great people, real or fictitious, offer abundant opportunities to mix virtue education with a variety of other subjects. We don't tell stories often enough any more, especially our own stories. When we do, virtue lessons come alive because all good stories relate to the existence of, struggle with, or absence of virtues.

30. **Contribution to school environment:** Whenever possible, see if you can plug something into a thematic unit activity that can contribute to other classes, other teachers, administrators, the janitor, or to the physical and aesthetic environment of the school. This not only opens doors for inserting lessons about character, but it also spreads the good vibrations of virtue practice throughout the school.

31. **Activism opportunity:** Our last technique or strategy recommendation for lesson plans that promote character education across the curriculum relates to activism. This is likely to be another controversial move on your part at one time or another. We know of a teacher in Idaho who was reprimanded for having students write letters in support of not shooting wolves from airplanes in Alaska. The reprimand came from a community with a contrary political opinion about wolves. When incorporating activism in your classroom at any age level, we recommend discussing both sides of the issue fairly and encouraging students to write letters or do projects in support of the side they agree with. Of course, our opinions may be influential, but this is unavoidable if we are as honest as we should be. Also, a universal virtue may guide the proper choice. Even if a local value supports one side of an issue, if the facts show that this value poisons rivers and air, for example, virtues should lead the way. Here, of course, is when walking the talk can become controversial.

Nonetheless, virtues-based activism is a way to walk the talk of critical thinking, reason, spirituality, generosity, and courage for everyone. It can be used in a variety of subject areas. It is no coincidence that environmental activists around the world have some key leaders who come from indigenous peoples. They know without doubt that we cannot continue to disrespect the earth or any of our relationships with others. Keeping a watchful eye on weather patterns, plants, and indicator species, they do not forget the damage people are doing, nor do they lose site of the challenges before us.

There are many opportunities for children to play a role. You may want to tell with them that the Wild Horse Act of 1978 that saved the mustangs from extinction was totally the result of the children across the United States whom "Wild Horse Annie" recruited to help with her campaign to save the horses!

Notes

1. Glasser, 1989, p. 22.

2. There will be sometimes, especially in the beginning of school, when you may want to concentrate on just the virtues, rather then blending them into core curriculum. The Council for Global Education has excellent booklets for children up to age 14, each of which offers teaching strategies for a particular virtue.

3. We found this quote in Tom Allen's excellent book, *Manager as Warrior*, published by Sinte Gleska University Press in 1993. Tom wrote this book in an effort to show how modern management on Lakota reservations does not have to forgo the traditional Lakota values for managers to be successful, and that, indeed, such values are paramount in all good.

4. These ideas about spirituality are controversial. Before our current publisher accepted our manuscript, another publisher's reviewer, an elementary school principal, had this to say about our approach to spirituality: "I find the their emphasis on 'spirituality' problematic and would have preferred they stayed with 'ethics.' In particular, I find the ideas about 'talking to trees' as an exercise

relating to expanding 'respect for all things' very difficult. I am sure such classroom instruction would be explosive, generating great resistance from students and parents."

5. Allen, 1993, p. 19.

6. Goleman, 1996, p. 86.

7. McLuhan, 1971, p. 57.

8. Caine, R. N., and Caine, G., 1997, p. 112.

9. When using critical thinking, it is important to include how the questions, such as "who benefits," be as related to global, ecological, and social perspectives as they are to individual, local ones. One critique of the critical pedagogy movement might be that it is still mired in individualistic outcomes.

Critical thinking is such an important part of character education that we tried to get a copy of this manuscript to Noam Chomsky at Massachusetts Institute of Technology. Dr. Chomsky is considered by many to be the world's most influential critical thinker. We were surprised and honored when we learned he read our manuscript and offered praise for the book.

10. As an international lecturer on hypnosis, a former professor at University of California–Berkeley who taught hypnosis for Marriage, Family, and Child Counselor licensure, and as author of several books on hypnosis, Jacobs can make this suggestion with some degree of wisdom.

11. Michael Cohen's book, *Reconnecting with Nature*, should be required reading in all classes. It offers practical ways for city-born and -raised youth to relate to nature as Indian people have done for thousands of years.

12. Mander, Winter 1997, p. 42.

13. John Seely Brown, director of the Xerox Palo Alto Research Center, and Paul Duguid, a resource specialists in social and cultural studies at University of California–Berkeley, wrote this book.

Chapter 4

Assessing a Virtues-Based Curriculum: The Process Is the Outcome

Edwin J. Dawson

> *In early days we were close to nature. We judged time, weather conditions,*
> *and many things by the elements—the good earth, the blue sky, the flying of geese,*
> *and the changing winds. We looked to these for guidance and answers.*
> *Today we are again evaluating the changing winds. May we*
> *be strong in spirit and equal to our Fathers of another day in reading the*
> *signs accurately and interpreting them wisely.*
> — speaker addressing the National Congress of American Indians in the mid-1960s,
> in Nabokov, *Native American Testimony*

> *The problems that exist in the world today cannot be solved*
> *by the level of thinking that created them.*
> — Albert Einstein (1979–1955), in *Adventures of a Mathematician*

In chapter 2, the authors briefly address some concerns about assessing, evaluating, and documenting the effects of teaching virtues across the curriculum. The questions surrounding assessment procedures are not novel, and all educators must address them whether the focus is geography, biology, or virtues. Ultimately any educational assessment boils down to answering one fundamental question: How much (if any) of what my students know, think, do, and believe can be attributed to what we have done together in the classroom? The answer to this question is essential to validate programs, modify objectives, rework lesson plans, and, yes, reevaluate assessment activities.

Since the now infamous series of articles was published concerning why Johnny or Janie can't read, write, etc., school systems at all levels have had to react to social and political pressures and devote resources to demonstrate that appropriate levels of academic expectations are being met. Unfortunately, the lion's share of proving academic success manifests itself as standardized tests, proportions of students exhibiting expected behaviors (i.e., enrolling in college, finding employment), and various other summative indices.[1] This is not surprising given our cultural obsession with competition. States, school districts, individual schools, instructors, and even students are caught up in the maelstrom of competing for status, space, awards, and funding. High stakes assessments demand a method of data gathering that can result in graphs, charts, percentiles, and other widely accepted means of proving who gets more, who gets punished, who gets rewarded, and who gets cut off. And through the continuous practice of hailing standardized assessments as the core method of measuring excellence, our educational system insidiously and covertly reinforces the virtue of categorizing, separating, establishing hierarchies, and divisiveness.

There is little wonder that character and virtue education curriculum have difficulty verifying their efficacy when the politically popular measure of valid supporting data rests with quantitative standardized instruments.[2] In truth, standardized tests have a place in educational assessment, albeit a narrow and nongeneralizable one. However, the decision rule for employing any assessment method must be driven by the *question* of interest, must match how the *content* is discussed, and must produce results in the most *useful* form to help instructors improve student learning.

This chapter on assessments for a virtue-based curriculum has two primary objectives. First, it discusses basic assumptions about the assessment of virtue education. Some of these assumptions are shared widely by education scholars and assessment specialists, while others are particular to this author and stem from decades of methodological study and practice. The second objective is to offer practical and tangible examples of how to design an assessment program for your class.

As is evident from the title of this chapter, our leitmotif is process as outcome. The cyclical nature of learning virtues, reflecting on virtues, applying virtues, connecting virtues, and discovering deeper understanding of the embeddedness of virtues in all of life, necessitates that as educators we track our success or failure by how we guide our students in their discovery. Focusing on traditional student outcomes (e.g., knowing a definition, coming to the right answer) distracts from the essential power of virtue-focused education, namely *transactional discovery* among teacher and students; students and students; students and family; and students, family, and community. Transactional discovery occurs when all parties interact and learn from one another. The process of transactional discovery *is* the outcome and should be the major focus of assessment activities.

Assumptions About Virtues-Based Curriculum Assessment

Assumption #1: Assessment and evaluation are related but different activities.

You probably learned this distinction in your sophomore methods class, yet I lead with it to stress the importance of a complete and well-organized assessment design. The process of assessment is to gather information about student learning systematically (or in this case, the transactional discovery) and use that information to communicate with students, parents, and others to improve learning and performance. Although this traditional definition under- and overdefines assessment by not specifically stressing the role of process assessment, and by over accentuating performance, it points to the importance of *systematically* gathering information across points in time that specifically relate to each other, build on each other, and ultimately construct a map that guides improvement of the process. Remember then, for an assessment program to be effective the logic undergirding each activity, when placed into the whole, points to areas of strength and weakness and anticipates methods for improvements.

The evaluation process uses the results of the assessments and makes *judgments* about student performance based on quality information gathered systematically over time. Judgments concerning virtues-based curriculum naturally will be based on whether a particular approach did or did not accomplish the intended affect, if activities stimulated self-reflection, if the level of attention to specific virtues was appropriate for grade-level and content, and if the teacher is effective in his or her role as guide. Judgments also must include determinations of how the process is to be improved, modified, reinforced, etc. (note Criteria Not Met "CNM" in the Sample Assessment Plan that follows). Built into the assessment design must be *a priori* decision rules on what, who, when, and whether to modify elements of the virtue curriculum. Try not to be caught saying, "Well, that didn't work. Now what?" Instead, be able to say, "Well, that didn't work. Let's go back and rework activity three since we knew before we started that if this unit didn't work, the problem would be in activity three." Know *how* you are going to use the assessment results to improve transactional discovery before you gather the information.

Assumption #2: The outcome is the process.

Assessment is not so much about judging, as it is about building. As I argued earlier in this chapter, the ultimate outcome of a virtue-based curriculum is how well the transactional discovery process works. The term *transactional discovery* warrants further discussion, since it derives from a general semantics paradigm that is perhaps not familiar to many. The term *transaction* is used in communication discipline to describe, in a more systemic and holistic manner, the process that occurs when individuals communicate. Instead of seeing that people interact sequentially (i.e., one talks, the other talks, the next talks, etc.), I prefer to think that people engage simultaneously in creating communication with each other. Effectiveness of communication, and, in our case, virtues education, occurs when all involved discover together the importance and applicability of virtues in our world. Each brings to the classroom his or her experiences, cultural beliefs, obtained knowledge, intuition, and concept of self. Along with the physical classroom environment, the messages shared, and the building of shared experiences, learning—or discover—occurs simultaneously among all involved.

Taking this perspective encourages assessment activities that investigate what happens during the transaction (process), not only what happened because of the interaction (outcome). Let me offer an example to clarify. Say I teach a one-week section on American history stressing the virtues of integrity, honesty, and courage. I incorporate a variety of role-play activities, private journal reflection, group projects, and class discussions. If I maintain the perspective of learning as an interaction among people, I would develop assessment activities to gather information on what the students learned at the end of the section or because of the classroom activities. If I change my focus to *transactional discovery* I develop assessment activities focused on how well the activities worked together to help the students and me discover how integrity, honesty, and courage relate to history and our immediate lives. I am less concerned with the end result of similar understanding of the virtues and more concerned that the experience helped self-discovery and self-reflection.

Assumption #3: Assessment plans must employ multiple methods and allow multiple opportunities for students and instructor-guides to demonstrate learning, discovery, and application.

Almost any assessment specialist will tout the importance of using multiple methods when gathering information about character and virtues education.[3] Unfortunately, many authors simply put forth a laundry list of data-gathering methods without explaining how to choose the appropriate method and, further, how to make sure that the information relates to the issue of interest.

Instead of attempting to discuss in this chapter, I tender a general rule for coordinating the results of multiple methods: *use clusters of methods that are based in similar assumptions*. For example, when assessing the depth with which students are able to relate virtues to situations, use a cluster of qualitative methods such as journal entries, personal interviews, and observation of small-group discussions. When evaluated through a rubric, the results of these three text-rich methods give a good indication of depth of understanding.

The journal allows students who do not like talking in groups a chance to demonstrate their understanding; the personal interview allows you to probe students in a nonthreatening atmosphere; and observing of a group discussion helps you discern how classmates collectively discover and learn from each other. This type of data triangulation paints one type of assessment picture. Do not mix quantitative methods with qualitative methods in a triangulation design. If you do, you end up reducing the text-rich descriptions to a number of categories that compare to numbers on a test. Equally as detrimental, you may make conclusions on how the numbers relate to the textual descriptions.

Designing an assessment plan around your favorite method or measurement technique will slant your results in that direction. Choose methods that match the construct of interest. For example, if the construct of interest is assessing a student's ability to self-reflect on the learning process, use the journal method. If the ability to use virtues in the decision-making process is of interest, then descriptive essay tests may be appropriate. If you want to apply virtues in action, role-play or nonparticipant observations may work.

Assumption #4: Effective assessment plans coordinate levels of measurement over time.

The assessment plan not only should incorporate multiple methods appropriate to the content and questions of interest, it also should organize three levels of measurement: immediate assessments, short-range markers, and long-range markers. Immediate assessment usually occurs during or after a classroom activity or class session. Gathering information at this point reflects the unmediated result or impression of the day's activities—students' enjoyment of the activity, learning the meaning of the concept, etc. Short-range markers assess the cumulative effect of a course segment or a planned period of time. These assessment activities usually are used to verify changes in students from one time to another. For example, before beginning a section on courage and fortitude, you assess the depth of their understanding of the terms and how they apply to math learning. After the four-week session is completed, you again assess the depth of student's understanding and ascertain whether changes meet with your expectations. Relating results from the short-term markers with the immediate assessments helps you understand how the four-week process may have influenced changes in perception. Examples of these types of assessments are displayed in the sample assessment plan section that follows.

Long-range markers are similar to short-range markers, but they attempt to gather information about learning, retention, growth, and application as a exponential, ever-increasing effect of the virtues-based curriculum, rather than simply an aggregate of the curriculum. More than simply longer periods of time between assessments, long-range markers solicit information from a wider constituency than just the students. Information from parents, administrators, family members, community members, and other relevant people that can assess the affects of the curriculum validly should be given an opportunity to mark program development.

Assumption #5: Students may be your best teachers on how to develop and integrate curriculum assessments.

In many educational settings, a shroud of mystery hangs over the assessment process. Lack of understanding of the process often results in anxiety, fear, resentment, and confusion. An essential part of assessing a virtues-based curriculum is to help your students understand what assessment is and how important it is for successful learning. (This lesson can fit easily with teaching the virtues of honesty, courage, patience, and humility.) One of the most significant long-range outcomes of a virtues-based curriculum is helping students to assess and reflect on their own decision rules.

It is important to establish an honest partnership with your students first, to assess the process openly, including your ability as teacher-guide, at any step along the journey. You may have a planned time to collect information, but if your students have something to say about the process, activity, or lesson, listen to them. Acknowledging and attending to their reflection on the process encourages them to participate in the discovery. Keep notes on what they focused on, how they measured it, and their suggestions for changes. Be sure to use the information in modifying your assessment plan and let your students know how their input has modified the program.

Assumption #6: Try as you might, you will never be able to assess completely the relationship between variables that influence and those that are influenced by teaching virtues in your classroom.

In other words, learn to live with incompleteness and ambiguity. The very nature of teaching virtues across the curriculum thrusts you into the world of holism, systems, and individual self-discovery. Linear thinking does not apply to these programs; therefore, clear-cut, standardized, compartmentalized, and empirically based assessments are not appropriate.[4] Choosing one easily identifiable and measurable variable and touting it as the representative indicator of program effectiveness is easy, but it undermines the very basis of holistic education.

The interrelatedness of components that comprise a virtues-based curriculum can never be determined fully because the process is being developed, changed, revised, and recreated constantly. As the system is altered (e.g., new virtues are introduced), the effect on students' understanding of humility may change, as will how humility relates to courage, and then fortitude . . . : In the face of this uncertainty, one may be tempted to forgo trying to assess the curriculum at all. At this point, remember that assessments are designed to collect systematically information that helps you improve the your classes. The onus is on you to determine, describe, and argue for the most important variables to assess *at this time and at this point in the process*. Will the variables of interest change? Of course. Will the relationship between variables change over time? Naturally. Will you ever know conclusively the effect your curriculum has on students, school and community? Probably not.

So, when you are asked to deliver a data-based summary of student learning to the public, including identification of program-wide strengths and weaknesses, and specific plans for using the information to improve learning (i.e., accountability), what will you report? I hope you will present first the assumptions underlying your curriculum and your assessment plan. Second, you may need to *educate* the public about the various types of information gathered to assess your virtues-based curriculum. In this context, your explanations of program strengths and weaknesses will make sense, and future plans for development will coincide with your primary objectives.

The bottom line on assessing your virtues-based curriculum is to know *why* you are assessing *what* your are assessing and *when* to change. Just as the important focus for assessing virtues-based education is process as outcome, the outcome of the assessment plan is improving the assessment process, as well. As in the opening quotation of this chapter, it is essential that as we evaluate the changing winds (i.e., the changes we hope to foster within our students and community), we read the signs accurately and interpret them wisely.

That the outcome is the process is supported in the following eight "Principles of Good Practice for Assessing Student Learning" set forth by the American Association of Higher Education. Notice that the AAHE stresses not only the concept of process, but also the inclusiveness of individuals when gathering data on the state of a program.

1. Assessment begins with virtues
2. Assessment is most effective when it reflects multidimensional, integrated, and revealed performance over time.
3. Assessment works best when a program has clearly stated purposes.
4. Assessment requires attention to the outcomes and experiences.
5. Assessment is best when it is ongoing, not episodic.
6. Assessment is better when representatives from across the education community are involved.
7. Assessment is best when it deals with issues people really care about.
8. Assessment is best when it is part of a larger set of conditions that promote change.

Example Assessment Plan

The following is a brief example of an assessment plan that relates to the curriculum plans in chapter 5. Materials from the lesson plan are in the center column and related discussions on the assessing activities are found in the left-hand column. The assessment activity is described in the right-hand column. This is intended only as a guide. You may want your initial development plan to be more elaborate. Following the Sample Assessment Plan are example questionnaires for parents, students, and teacher/staff. These questionnaires are only an example to guide your own construction of short-range assessment tools.[5]

During the first week of the school year it is important that you inform all teachers and staff who come in contact with your students, and your student's parents, that you will need their input in helping you assess (or evaluate) the extent to which your virtues-based curriculum is working. How you solicit cooperation from these relevant parties depends on whether virtues education has been officially adopted across your school, grade, or department. In any case, you should give each constituency a brief background of the program, objectives of your assessment plan, and how and when you will call on them for their opinions. Included in the information letter should be specific areas of process (and outcome) of interest to you (e.g., honesty, courage, humility, patience).

One effect that may be evidenced is behavioral indices across classes. The process of teaching virtues in your class through small-group activities *should* influence the small-group activities in other classes. In this way, a fellow teacher's observations that students are becoming more *patient* and *cooperative* during small-group activities may show that overtly discussing and commenting on patience and cooperation during class activities has affected student's behaviors.

SAMPLE ASSESSMENT PLAN

Discussion	Section	Assessment Activity and Method
	(Refer to Chapter 5: American History Lesson)	
Writing clear objectives that guide your assessment plan helps maintain your focus when developing activities. The objectives also can be used to explain your intentions to the "public." Notice the specificity of the type of activity, the method for collecting information, and how the data will/can be used to improve learning.	**Thematic Unit Week 1: Discrimination** Academic: *Students will be able to demonstrate knowledge of the events surrounding the "Trail of Tears," in terms of government, economics, law, and discrimination, and identify current issues of discrimination issues that may be similar.* Character: *Students will be able to demonstrate an understanding of how discrimination can be reduced or ended by people who exhibit courage, honesty, humility, generosity, and fortitude as features of their character.*	Assessment A (day 1): one-page paper describing what factors caused people to discriminate against immigrants in the first half, and what character virtues might have prevented. Criteria not met (CNM): Modify opening questions. Assessment B (day 3): three paragraphs, one each describing an interview with a family or community member. CNM: check explanation of assignment. Assessment C (day 4): test to identify discrimination and student explanations of why having courage can keep people from discriminating against others. CNM: use day to summarize major concepts. Observational Assessments (days 2 and 3): Note examples of patience, fortitude, and generosity as students work together on the computer, and during role-play. Examples of honest sharing about their reactions to discrimination stories.
Continue recording each Unit's Objectives and Corresponding Assessment Activities. Make special note of the method of assessment, time, and focus of each activity.	**Thematic Unit Week 2: Exploration** Academic Objectives: *Students will be able to demonstrate . . .* Character Objectives: *Students will be able to demonstrate an understanding of . . .*	Assessment A (day 3): small-group discussion of issues relevant to topic and school. Assessment B (day 4): matching test on character issues and depictions of virtues in action.

SAMPLE ASSESSMENT PLAN (continued)

Discussion	Section	Assessment Activity and Method
CONTINUE RECORDING	THEMATIC UNITS 3–8	ASSESSMENT FOR UNITS 3–8
Short-range assessment	Quarterly Teacher/Staff Assessment (see example)	Distribute Teacher Questionnaire to all teachers who contact your students. Include relevant staff. Ask each to complete the questionnaire and return to you within a week.
Short-range assessment: remember always to note students' comments about activities, methods, etc., and keep daily written notes.	Quarterly Student Assessment (see example on page 115)	Distribute student self-reflection questionnaire as a two-day take-home activity. Give the students the "2 × 2" classroom assessment graph to complete during class time.
Short-range assessment	Quarterly Parent Guardian Assessment (see example)	Mail Parent/Guardian Assessment (do not send home with student). Include self-addressed, stamped return envelope.
CONTINUE RECORDING	THEMATIC UNITS 9–END	ASSESSMENT FOR UNITS 9–END
Short-range assessment: at this point you may want to solicit direct recommendations from fellow teachers.	Mid-Year Teacher/Staff Assessment (see example)	Distribute Teacher Questionnaire to all teachers who contact your students. Include relevant staff. Ask each to complete the questionnaire and return to you within a week.
Short-range assessment: you may replace the 2 × 2 graph with personal interviews with students on similar topics.	Mid-Year Student Assessment (see example)	Distribute student self-reflection questionnaire as a two-day take-home activity. Give the students the "2 × 2" classroom assessment graph to complete during class time.
Short-range assessment: you may arrange to discuss parent responses during student-teacher meetings.	Mid-Year Parent/Guardian Assessment (see example)	Mail Parent/Guardian Assessment (do not send home with student) include self-addressed, stamped return envelope.

QUARTERLY TEACHER/STAFF ASSESSMENT

Date

Dear Teacher or Staff Member of "Our School":

I am interested in your opinion regarding my virtues curriculum for our 10th grade Social Studies class and the effects the program may have on our students. Please take a few minutes to complete this questionnaire. Including your name is not necessary, but you may record it on this sheet if you would like.

Thank you for taking an interest in our students and this program.

1. In your opinion, over the past two months (or whatever time frame is appropriate) what *positive* changes (if any) have you noticed in our 10th graders with regard to the following items:

    Courageousness (i.e., venturing into unfamiliar territory, taking positive risks, telling the complete story, etc.)

Great Change	Moderate Change	Little Change	No Change
○	○	○	○

    Fortitude (i.e., sticking to worthwhile tasks, self-discipline, not taking the easy way out, attaining goals, etc.)

Great Change	Moderate Change	Little Change	No Change
○	○	○	○

    Patience (not easily provoked, takes time to listen, accept frustrations without giving up, etc.)

Great Change	Moderate Change	Little Change	No Change
○	○	○	○

    Honesty (caring about the truth, doing what they say, being trustworthy)

Great Change	Moderate Change	Little Change	No Change
○	○	○	○

    Humility (lack of arrogance, recognize and demonstrate equality and equity)

Great Change	Moderate Change	Little Change	No Change
○	○	○	○

    Generosity (giving and sharing of their time, ideas, unselfish sharing of their resources)

Great Change	Moderate Change	Little Change	No Change
○	○	○	○

    Responsibility

Great Change	Moderate Change	Little Change	No Change
○	○	○	○

    Attitude toward School

Great Change	Moderate Change	Little Change	No Change
○	○	○	○

Attitude toward teachers

Great Change	Moderate Change	Little Change	No Change
○	○	○	○

Attitude toward School work

Great Change	Moderate Change	Little Change	No Change
○	○	○	○

2. Have you heard our students talking about virtues, character, or any of the above items in or out of the classroom?

   ○   Yes, quite a bit
   ○   Yes, a few times
   ○   Yes, but not often
   ○   No, I don't recall them talking about virtues

Please elaborate on your responses with examples.

_____

_____

_____

_____

_____

_____

_____

_____

_____

QUARTERLY PARENT/GUARDIAN ASSESSMENT

Date

Dear Parent or Guardian:

I am interested in your opinions regarding the effects of the virtues curriculum your daughter or son is learning in my Social Studies class. Please take a few minutes to complete this questionnaire and return it in the self-addressed, stamped envelope. Including your name is not necessary, but you may record it on this sheet if you would like.

Thank you for assisting me in developing an effective curriculum for your child.

1. In your opinion, over the past two months (or whatever time frame is appropriate) what *positive* changes (if any) have you noticed in your daughter or son with regard to the following items:

   Courageousness (i.e., venturing into unfamiliar territory, taking positive risks, telling the complete story, etc.)

Great Change	Moderate Change	Little Change	No Change
○	○	○	○

   Fortitude (i.e., sticking to worthwhile tasks, self-discipline, not taking the easy way out, attaining goals, etc.)

Great Change	Moderate Change	Little Change	No Change
○	○	○	○

   Patience (not easily provoked, takes time to listen, accept frustrations without giving up, etc.)

Great Change	Moderate Change	Little Change	No Change
○	○	○	○

   Honesty (caring about the truth, doing what they say, being trustworthy)

Great Change	Moderate Change	Little Change	No Change
○	○	○	○

   Humility (lack of arrogance, recognize and demonstrate equality and equity)

Great Change	Moderate Change	Little Change	No Change
○	○	○	○

   Generosity (giving and sharing of their time, ideas, unselfish sharing of their resources)

Great Change	Moderate Change	Little Change	No Change
○	○	○	○

   Responsibility

Great Change	Moderate Change	Little Change	No Change
○	○	○	○

   Attitude toward School

Great Change	Moderate Change	Little Change	No Change
○	○	○	○

Attitude toward teachers

Great Change	Moderate Change	Little Change	No Change
○	○	○	○

Attitude toward School work

Great Change	Moderate Change	Little Change	No Change
○	○	○	○

2. Have you heard your daughter or son talking about virtues, character, or any of the above items at home or with her or his friends?

- ○ Yes, quite a bit
- ○ Yes, a few times
- ○ Yes, but not often
- ○ No, I don't recall them talking about virtues

Please elaborate on your responses with examples.

_____

_____

_____

_____

_____

_____

_____

_____

_____

_____

QUARTERLY STUDENT 2 × 2 ASSESSMENT

Date

For the past two months (or whatever time frame is appropriate) we have been learning about virtues through our Social Studies topics. I have noticed how you've reacted to some of the activities and the assignments. I always consider your comments when developing lesson plans.

Now, I am asking you for some specific reactions to our classes.

In the 2 × 2 matrix below I would like you to write down any comments about the types of things we have or have not been doing in our class. For example, in the upper-left box, write down those things that we have been doing that you like and would like us to do more of. In the upper-right hand box, write down things you think we should stop doing.

	START DOING	**STOP DOING**
MORE OF		
LESS OF		

1. Over the past two months (or whatever time frame is appropriate) what *positive* changes (if any) have you noticed in the way you think about or behave, considering the following areas:

Courageousness (i.e., venturing into unfamiliar territory, taking positive risks, telling the complete story, etc.)

Great Change	Moderate Change	Little Change	No Change
○	○	○	○

Please explain in your own words:

_____

_____

_____

Fortitude (i.e., sticking to worthwhile tasks, self-discipline, not taking the easy way out, attaining goals, etc.)

Great Change	Moderate Change	Little Change	No Change
○	○	○	○

Please explain in your own words:

_____

_____

_____

Patience (not easily provoked, takes time to listen, accepts frustrations without giving up, etc.)

Great Change	Moderate Change	Little Change	No Change
○	○	○	○

Please explain in your own words:

_____

_____

_____

Honesty (caring about the truth, doing what you say, being trustworthy)

Great Change	Moderate Change	Little Change	No Change
○	○	○	○

Please explain in your own words:

_____

_____

_____

Humility (lack of arrogance, recognize and demonstrate equality and equity)

Great Change	Moderate Change	Little Change	No Change
○	○	○	○

Please explain in your own words:

_____

_____

_____

Generosity (giving and sharing of your time, ideas, unselfish sharing of your resources)

Great Change	Moderate Change	Little Change	No Change
○	○	○	○

Please explain in your own words:

_____

_____

_____

Responsibility

Great Change	Moderate Change	Little Change	No Change
○	○	○	○

Please explain in your own words:

_____

_____

_____

Attitude toward school

Great Change   Moderate Change   Little Change   No Change
○   ○   ○   ○

Please explain in your own words:

_____

_____

_____

Attitude toward teachers

Great Change   Moderate Change   Little Change   No Change
○   ○   ○   ○

Please explain in your own words:

_____

_____

_____

Attitude toward school work

Great Change   Moderate Change   Little Change   No Change
○   ○   ○   ○

Please explain in your own words:

_____

_____

_____

2. Do you talk about virtues, character, or any of the above items at home or with your friends?

   ○   Yes, quite a bit
   ○   Yes, a few times
   ○   Yes, but not often
   ○   No, I don't recall them talking about virtues

Please explain your response:

_____

_____

_____

Notes

1. For good synopses of assessment practices, see: Guerin, and Maier, 1983; For a concise article on methods for determining success of learners, see Herman, et al., 1992. A practical guide to alternative assessment, Alexandria, Va.: ASCD Publications.

2. For an excellent start to locating assessment tools for short- and long-range evaluations, go to *http://www.character.org/search2/index.cgi*, the assessment search engine for the Character Education Partnership. As in any assessment activity, choose the method based on the question of interest and usefulness of the results.

3. Multiple methods of collecting data are a common direction in educational research. For an overview, see Brewer et al., 1999.

4. Assessing a virtues-based curriculum (e.g., character education) is fraught with methodological concerns, among which are the ability to tease out the impact of teaching virtues from other mediating influences and observed behaviors as temporary responses and not deep-rooted virtue changes. For discussions on methodological problems, see Cline and Feldmesser, 1983; Pritchard, 1988, pp. 469–93.

5. Items on these questionnaires are based on content found in assessment tools from De-Roche and Williams, 1998.

Appendix

CHARACTER DEVELOPMENT PLAN — PART I
1998–2001

IRVING B. WEBER ELEMENTARY
3850 Rohret Road
Iowa City, Iowa 52246
319-339-5757
FAX 319-339-5763

Above all, remember that the meaning of life is
to build a life as if it were a work of art.
— Abraham Joshua Heschel, *The Basic School: A Community for Learning*

At Weber Elementary students become knowledgeable in many curricular areas and strive to become socially and ethically responsible. To that end the curriculum includes a commitment to character development by focusing on seven essential human qualities of character development, called core virtues: honesty, respect, responsibility, compassion, self-control, perseverance, and giving. Parents as the first teachers of their children establish these virtues at home, and the school reinforces and supports these teachings.

Character Education in Our School

As a Basic School, Weber Elementary "is concerned with the ethical and moral dimensions of a child's life. The goal is to assure that all students, on leaving school, will have developed a keen sense of personal and civic responsibility. Seven core virtues, such as respect, compassion, and perseverance, are emphasized to guide the Basic School as it promotes excellence in living, as well as learning"[1] (Boyer, 1994).

The character education programming at Irving B. Weber Elementary School is a systemic approach. It is deeply rooted in the curriculum and in the life of the learning community. The works of Dr. Ernest Boyer and Eric Schaps have heavily influenced our approach. We share Dr. Boyer's vision to "help each child build a life as if it were a work of art." The four priorities of the Basic School help us to integrate character development into our curriculum and into the home/school connection and the broader community. The four priorities are:

* community for learning,
* curriculum with coherence,
* climate for learning, and
* commitment to character.

We strive to teach the core virtues of the Basic School through word and deed. These virtues represent values that are held by any orderly society, and they transcend the artificial boundaries that can separate us.

In partnership, parents and teachers promote students in "discovering lessons in virtue across the whole curriculum . . . through the curriculum, through school climate, and through service."[2] The Basic School framework addresses character education through the learning community with community considered to be the foundation for learning. Our families and staff come from diverse cultural, racial, and ethnic backgrounds; yet, children and adults share a common vision and language of the Basic School. Education in moral and ethical decision making and service to others takes place in the home, the classroom, and the community. Helping children become compassionate, ethical citizens is a shared community responsibility. We are committed to teaching and modeling ethical and moral behavior in our own daily lives and in our curriculum. Building children's lives as works of art also requires us to see and recreate our own lives as works of art.

The Weber staff and parents believe deeply that character education involves head, heart, and hands. What we know, think, and feel ultimately is translated into the actions of our lives. Therefore, character education must be interwoven into the curriculum and the life of the school, not reduced to a list of behaviors or prescribed lessons. Student involvement is at the heart of character development programming that is not mediated by adults only. Students participate in school decisions, projects, leadership, and volunteerism. They learn processes for decision making, resolving conflict, teaming, and serving. Students initiate service projects as they learn of needs. Children have raised funds for the regional Children's Museum, the Domestic Violence and Emergency Housing Centers, Ronald McDonald House, and other community needs. They collect books for children and supplies for disaster areas. Students catalog, archive, and display art and artifacts in the Weber School Cultural Heritage Museum; others serve on Student Council. Many act as Media Center and lunchroom helpers, managers of the School Store, conflict resolution managers, patrols, mentors and tutors, and hosts and ambassadors for the school. All children nurture their "buddies" through the all-school buddy classes that match older and younger children in "buddy" activities throughout the year.

Children and adults process daily how to act and live together in harmony and in service to others. Children's and adults' acts of kindness can be seen many times during the course of a day. These acts are not random, however; they are intentional because children and adults see needs and act without prompting.

Eric Schaps, president of the Developmental Studies Center, reminds us that if children's basic needs of belonging and feeling competent are met, they are more motivated and inclined to accept and internalize the values that we teach and model. We use the Basic School framework to address these basic needs by

- building a strong **community** where children have a voice and have strong connections with peers and adults;
- developing an **integrated curriculum** that engages children in purposeful learning activities that have meaning for them, that promote competence, that incorporate critical thinking, and that help them internalize the core virtues;
- creating a **climate for learning** where resources and structures match the aims of the school; and
- fulfilling a **commitment to character** by nurturing children to be compassionate, critical thinkers who live by a set of moral and ethical principles and who initiate service to the community.

Weaving together a curriculum tapestry using one or more of the eight commonalties of the Basic School, teaching teams write and teach integrated units. That tapestry includes content skills, ethical and moral questions and behaviors related to the disciplines and topics, exemplars of core virtues, and opportunities for community service. Through the curriculum and the school climate, we help students to experience and value independent moral reasoning by emphasizing projects and performance assessment. Open-ended questions, projects, investigations, and leadership opportunities promote autonomy, reflection, and moral reasoning. Children are encouraged to apply the lessons of the classroom to the world around them and to be engaged in meaningful reflection, decision making, and leadership.

Strategies for Character Development

A variety of strategies promote character development. One of them is a character development rubric, which rubric is useful in several ways. It provides a basis for understanding the meaning of the virtues through observable behaviors. Such behaviors are placed on a continuum of levels. Three of the four levels are considered acceptable in terms of developmental behavioral expectations. However, each student is encouraged to strive toward higher levels of social development based on his or her maturity. This development is a reflection of progress in overall character development.

Using the rubric, students, teachers, and parents are able to solve specific problems and ascertain levels of behavior related to character development at any particular point. Knowing one's level of character development or performance is very important when problem solving and goal setting with individuals or with groups of students. Useful goals may be determined using the rubric as a tool to measure progress toward performance at higher levels. All people have good days and bad days, but thoughtful and regular use of the model will help students to reflect on their actions and identify meaningful behavioral patterns useful for facilitating growth of character development and programming.

The model enables teachers to develop effective instructional strategies designed to help students understand and apply the model regularly. These strategies are positive in conception and application, and they help character development become an integrated part of the intentional teaching and learning process.

Core Virtues

- Honesty
- Respect
- Responsibility
- Compassion
- Self-discipline
- Perseverance
- Giving

I-Care Rules

Enforcing I-Care Rules ensures that all students develop a sense of personal and civic responsibility. As a community of learners, our students learn and model I-Care Rules, which are all equally important. These rules encourage positive character development and encompass all the core virtues of the Basic School. They are taught, reviewed, and practiced throughout the school year in Team 1 (5- to 6-year-olds) and Team 2 (8- to 10-year-olds).

I-CARE RULES
- We listen to each other.
- Hands are for helping, not hurting.
- We use I Care language.
- We care about each other's feelings.
- We are responsible for what we say and do.
- Different is OK.

Put Yourself in Charge

Put Yourself in Charge is another set of strategies also used by all students at Weber to promote positive behavior. This approach helps students to understand that people have control over many events in their environment. When someone becomes annoyed with another person's behavior, four simple chronological steps should be taken to manage the annoying behavior: ignore it, ask that it be stopped, walk away from it, or report it to the adult teacher/supervisor. Once students learn and practice these four steps, they will be able to solve many of their own problems.

PUT YOURSELF IN CHARGE
- Ignore
- Ask to stop
- Walk away
- Report

Implementing Core Virtue Actions Plans

The staff at Irving B. Weber Elementary is committed to teaching and modeling the core virtues of the Basic School: honesty, respect, responsibility, compassion, self-discipline, perseverance, and giving. We use many strategies to encourage positive character development in each of these areas, we also realize that there are times when children may have difficulty displaying these virtues. We have developed a plan to handle student behaviors that do not reflect core virtues. The process and steps are:

- Tell the student that the behavior is not acceptable and discuss how that virtue is not being addressed appropriately.
- Separate the student from the problem, again discussing the student's action and the core virtues.
- Remove the child from the situation and discuss the activity.
- Complete a Core Virtue Action Plan* with the student to share with the student, parent, principal, or any variation of the three.

*See attached Core Virtue Action Plan and Core Virtue Rubrics.

CORE VIRTUE ACTION PLAN

Student's Name _____ Homeroom Teacher _____

Date _____ Time _____

Description of Problem to Be Solved/Comments:

_____

_____

_____

_____

_____

	Core Virtue (See Rubric)	**Student Action Plan**
1. Honesty		
2. Respect:		
3. Responsibility:		
4. Compassion:		
5. Self-Discipline:		
6. Perseverance:		
7. Giving:		

Our school character development plan focuses on the Weber Basic School core virtues listed at the top of this page. We have prepared this plan with your child to keep you informed and to maintain productive home/ school communications. Your child has been asked to return this form with your signature on the next school day. Thank you for reviewing it with your child.

Student _____ Teacher _____

Principal _____ Parent _____

CHARACTER DEVELOPMENT PLAN — Part II
RUBRICS
Irving B. Weber Elementary Character Development Rubric

CORE VIRTUES	HONESTY	RESPECT	RESPONSIBILITY	COMPASSION	SELF-DISCIPLINE	PERSEVERANCE	GIVING
Levels of Commitment: Responsibility for self and others (Level 4)	Is trustworthy. Is supportive of others and helps others take responsibility for their actions and work. Independently takes some risk in sharing ideas openly.	Supports others with positive comments. Helps others and self to follow directions. Willing works with a group.	Conscientiously performs and accepts tasks willingly. Displays ownership for work completed and any actions. Dependable.	Considerate, forgiving, and caring. Acknowledges other people's feelings and offers comfort.	Reflects habits of good living in all aspects of life. Develops and meets individual and group goals and disciplines.	Encourages others to complete tasks. Sets challenging goals and sustains strong commitment to them.	Receives satisfaction from sharing with others. Initiates service activities. Seeks opportunities to respond positively to needs of others without regard or recognition.
Involvement (Level 3)	Takes responsibility for own actions and work. Takes some risk in sharing ideas with encouragement from others.	Makes positive comments and "put ups" some of the times. Willingly works with a partner. Listens and attends to others.	Offers positive input to others and to situations.	Is aware of others' feelings and responds to their needs.	Models appropriate behaviors and recognizes expectations.	Completes tasks.	Willingly shares ideas, materials, or time. Participates in service activities (intrinsic motivation)
In Control (Level 2)	With some encouragement and support from others, takes responsibility for own actions and work.	With some reminders, keeps self from calling others names, striking or pushing others; using negative comments, negative body language, or "put downs." Allows others to listen and pay attention.	With some encouragement, keeps self from performing negative acts—acting out.	Is aware of others' feelings but ignores them.	With some encouragement, lives within limits and is accepting of those guidelines.	Makes an attempt.	Will share ideas, materials, or time when given a reward. (extrinsic motivation)
Irresponsibility (Level 1)	Does not take responsibility for own actions or work. Denies any wrongdoing. Does not tell the truth.	Calls people names. Strikes or pushes others. Uses negative comments, negative body language, or "put downs."	Does not take ownership for negative actions or words.	Hurtful, with little or no regard for how others feel.	Acts out in a disruptive manner that is harmful to self and others.	Gives up quickly or doesn't try.	Does not share time, materials, or ideas with others.

CORE VIRTUES RUBRIC

Honesty • acknowledges wrongdoing • shares ideas openly			
Respect • treats people and property in a positive manner • realizes that different is OK • accepts constructive criticism			
Compassion • is caring and considerate • reaches out to others • seeks reconciliation • tries to understand and forgive			
Perseverance • strength and determination to pursue goals • diligence • pushes hard to complete assignments			
Giving • shares talents through service • responds positively to the needs of others			
Self-Discipline • lives within limits/expectations • controls the way interacts with others			
Responsibility • willing sense of duty to complete tasks • accountable for behavior			

CARE RULES RUBRIC

1. We listen to each other. (respect)			
2. Hands are for helping, not hurting. (self-discipline/giving)			
3. We use I-Care language. (honesty/respect/compassion)			
4. We care about each other's feelings. (compassion/respect)			
5. We are responsible for what we say and do. (responsibility/honesty)			
6. Different is OK. (respect/compassion)			

Notes

1. Boyer, 1994.
2. ———, 1995.

Part 3
The Interconnections of the South

Chapter 5

Social Studies, of Course!

We were lawless people, but we were on pretty good terms with the Great Spirit.
When people live far from scenes of the Great Spirit's making,
it is easy for them to forget His laws.
— Walking Buffalo, in McLuhan's *Touch the Earth*

The only way to implement our good vision of society is
to bring it down to a vision of a single household.
— Chongyam Trungpa, *Sacred Path of the Warrior*

We begin our sample lesson plans with the subject most people think is a natural for integrating character education into content. Indeed, one would think that the study of social institutions and practices would be indivisible from the study of virtues. Yet in our fragmented, objectified education system, even the social sciences ignore character education. Marker and Mehlinger's review of the social studies curriculum concluded that "the apparent consensus that citizenship education is the primary purpose of social studies is almost meaningless."[1]

If social studies teachers do discuss moral issues while learning about such subjects as government, sociology, history, or economics, they target how people are expected to *behave*, rather than how people should *be*. They tend to rationalize the status quo rather than attempt to transform it into something better. The focus turns to rules, not personhood. Moreover, many social studies teachers tend to present moral rules or expectations as concrete guidelines that are unique to the values of the particular culture. This can exclude or even contradict more universal perspectives about virtue.

In our lesson plan examples, we suggest a different view and recommend using universally acknowledged virtues to assess social institutions and crossing all boundaries to do so. We believe students should be able to incorporate their unique cultural backgrounds into this assessment, along with dialogue that brings into context comparisons and contrasts with universal understanding about the virtues. We do not endorse an ethical relativism that asserts that morality is based on the norms of one's culture. Societies' moral practices may differ, but the fundamental moral principles underlying the practices do not. People may have different views on capital punishment, for example, but still agree that it is wrong to commit murder. Cultures may have practices that violate their basic moral principles (and capital punishment may be an example also), and still know that these practices are morally wrong.

This sense of universality makes teaching social studies with character education in mind easy and exciting. The study of universally honored virtues keeps us from focusing too much on what people *should* do or how they *should* act. This helps minimize an overemphasis on compliance with external local authority. Rather, character education helps us concentrate on the kind of people human beings can become by teaching the character traits that develop our inherent positive potentials. A person trained to follow the mandates of authority or the authority's rules for the sake of obedience, and who has not internalized the universal virtues, too easily follows unhealthy or destructive mandates.[2] To avoid using character education as merely another tool for control and compliance, great care must be taken to ensure that teachable moments for developing character are not merely opportunities for classroom control and obedience.

Even more significant to social studies than the sense of universal virtues is the fact that at the heart of virtues training is the idea of community. Character is not developed in isolation, but within and with family, church, school, and other associations. Hence, social sciences and history provide an ideal arena for mixing content standards with virtue objectives and processes such as service learning or social and environmental activism.[3]

Sample Lesson Plan, Grade Level 5

The content standard we have selected for this lesson is California Social Science and History Standard 5.3, #4: "the role of broken treaties and massacres and the factors that led to the Indians' defeat, including the resistance of Indian nations to encroachments and assimilation (e.g., the story of the Trail of Tears)." The theme we have chosen to make our unit meaningful to our student's lives is *discrimination*. We borrowed the original framework for this lesson plan from Mike Koren, a middle school teacher at Maple Dale School in Fox Point, Wisconsin.[4] We took his original lesson plan, plugged everything into our format, used the Pedagogy and Procedures Checklist to modify or add teaching strategies that would open doors for relevant character education, and then looked for natural opportunities to embed virtues education and underlined them in additional notes. Since a part of this lesson refers to the atrocities of humans, it is important to be sensitive to student reactions and stay focused on the role of virtues or their absence. This lesson probably should not be used with younger children.

Instructional Procedures for Day 1

1. Ask the opening questions and allow students to close their eyes and contemplate the answers (7, 8, 17, 20). *(Note to reader:[5] Take a moment to note why each of these strategies from the Pedagogy and Procedures Checklist is noted. Why might using them make it easier to create opportunities for virtue awareness? In particular, how would the visualization exercise make associations between the subject and virtues relevant to the individual student's life?)*

   Then ask each student to write down his or her own definition of discrimination *using one of the virtues in the definition.* (17). *(Note to reader: Remember, we are underlining teachable virtues education moments for later reference.)*

   Divide students into small groups and ask them to agree on a definition for discrimination and to choose *which virtue is most likely helpful for preventing it.* They can use the dictionary, but ask them to put the definition in their own words. After about 5–10 minutes, each group shares its definition, and we agree on a definition everyone likes. (1, 5, 15, 16, 23). *(Note to reader: If you are instructing student teachers in this process, ask them to explain why each of the numbers has been selected from the checklist.)*

   Then, tell my favorite ethnic joke (20, 25). *(Note to reader: Use age-appropriate discretion and clarification here. Using such humor often stimulates ideas that bring into play an awareness of spiritual connections and relevant virtues practice.)*

LESSON PLAN FORMAT

Title: Discrimination	Learning Goals	Official Content Standard Addressed
• Academic subject: *American history* • Character subject: *Courage, honesty, humility, fortitude, generosity* • Grade levels: *10–12* • Time allowed: *Four days* • Date last modified: *6-21-00*	Academic: *Students will gain a critical awareness of the true history of Indian and white relationships before the Civil War and have a basic understanding of the role discrimination played and continues to play in the U.S. regarding relationships with people of different cultural backgrounds.* Character: *Students will gain an understanding of how virtues or their absence might have played into the history of U.S. relations with Indians, and how discrimination affects these students' personal lives.*	*California History/Social Science Content Standards, Grade 5: U.S. History: Making a New Nation, 5.3, #4; Students describe the cooperation and conflict that existed among the Indians and between the Indian nations and the new settlers, in terms of: "the role of broken treaties and massacres and the factors that led to the Indians' defeat, including the resistance of Indian nations to encroachments and assimilation (e.g., the story of the Trail of Tears)."*

Specific Objectives	Resources and Materials
Academic: *Students will be able to demonstrate knowledge of the events surrounding the "Trail of Tears," in terms of government, economics, law, and discrimination, and identify current discrimination that may be similar.* Character: *Students will be able to demonstrate an understanding of how discrimination can be reduced or ended by people with courage, honesty, humility, generosity, and fortitude as strong features of their character.*	*Internet access and addresses for information on the Cherokee Trail of Tears and the German Holocaust; the video, The Immigrant Experience—Long, Long Journey; the book, Native American Testimony, the video on prejudice against black people in the south; list of examples and non-examples of discrimination.*

Student Prerequisite Skills/Knowledge	Opening Questions
Academic: *Ability to do research on the Web and work in groups* Character: *Can offer a working definition of the six core virtues*	Academic: *What similarities are there between the holocaust, the treatment of immigrants to the United States, the experience of blacks in the south during the 1960s, and government policies toward the American Indian in the early 1800s? How are things similar or different today?* Character: *If most of the people in authority or those who followed their orders were of good character—that is, consistently true to the tenants of courage, honesty, generosity and fortitude—might the history of these atrocities be different?*

For example: An Asian couple adopted a black boy and a white boy. All their lives the parents and the children debated about whether God was white, black, or yellow. The debate was always respectful, and all loved one another deeply, but they were obsessed with the discussion. After the parents passed on, the children, now grown men, continued the speculation well into old age. When they were in their 80s, they both died on the same day and went to heaven. When they arrived, the first thing they wanted to know was whether God was black, white, or yellow. The gatekeeper said to them, "Well, go see for yourself." They went around the corner and looked inside the great room where God resided. When he saw them, He said, *Hau!* (Lakota for hello . . . God was obviously a "red man." They were all wrong.) *Telling the joke will provide sufficient levity to increase levels of courage to talk about different groups of people in later discussions.*

2. Tell the students: Today and tomorrow in class, we will watch a video about a Polish child being harassed as he tries to assimilate into U.S. culture, another video about some young black people who were beaten and murdered by the Ku Klux Klan in the South during the '60s, and you will use the Internet to learn about the Trail of Tears. You will also read a few stories told by Indians who lived in the early 1800s (29). *(Note to reader: Story telling is always an excellent way to illustrate important virtues, and this is especially true in most American Indian stories.)*

   As you study the films, do the Internet research, and read the speeches, please consider the similarities between them and any related issues in your own community. Be prepared to discuss a minimum of five such issues with the class (20, 24). *(Note to reader: Although too many movies and too much television is probably more harmful than good, powerful images in film, when followed by meaningful dialogue, can help plant seeds for good character in young people.)*

3. Show selected parts of the video about the immigrant experience. Then divide students into groups (1) and have them discuss and write down four specific acts of discrimination from the film, including who did them, and why they think the acts happened, and how they think the acts made the Polish boy feel. (6, 7, 23, 20). *Then ask them to identify how and when someone in the video either displayed or did not display one of the virtues (courage, fortitude, honesty, humility, or generosity). (Note to reader: Just a reminder that we are underlining references to virtues so we can use them later to assess how often we teach virtues and what strategies can be used in other lessons that were successful.)*

4. Homework: Write a one-page paper describing what factors caused people to discriminate against immigrants in the first half, and *what character virtues might have prevented the same people from acting this way.* It will be graded (4). *(Note to reader: We believe the "extrinsic motivation" strategy needs to be used once in a while, but only minimally. Intrinsic motivation is much more conducive to effective teaching of virtues. However, by using traditional grading and relating it to virtues education, an interesting increase in credibility for the subject happens for those who associate "serious" subject matter with grading.)*

Instructional Procedures for Day 2

1. Assign groups of two or three students to each of the computers and tell them to find out everything they can about the removal of the Cherokee and Creek Indians from Georgia during what became known as "The Trail of Tears." Also hand out copies of the Indian stories relating to that event. Tell them each group will pair with another to

create a 10-minute drama depicting this event (6, 9, 29). Groups will be assessed on how thorough their research was based on what is presented. *Ask students to compare and contrast degrees of courage needed to perform in front of a group with that needed by the Indians to survive the Trail of Tears. Talk about the many forms of courage.*

2. Acknowledge the students who are working diligently on the research (3). *(Note to reader: Acknowledgment is a way to elicit intrinsic motivation, whereas praise is generally extrinsic.) Also acknowledge the display of patience, fortitude, and generosity as you observe the students working together on the computer. It is likely all three will bear on the work.* Help students with the research as needed (12). When some of the truly tragic parts of the story are revealed, ask the students if they feel strong emotions about what happened and how they are resolving those emotions (10). *Ask if they are being honest about their reactions to the discrimination stories they have heard thus far.*

3. Homework: Call members of your group and work out the script for your role-play tomorrow.

Instructional Procedures for Day 3

1. Have the groups act out The Trail of Tears (9, 15). As they do, ask questions to ensure that students know the historical facts regarding the U.S. president's ignoring the Supreme Court decision, land issues, support for the Indians by non-Indians, and inhumanity and injustice of the forced eviction (6, 9).

2. Show selected parts of the video on the treatment of blacks in the South during the 1960s. If there is time, have each student visualize being one of the people he or she has learned about being discriminated against and get in touch with the resulting feelings. Then have each student imagine the same person being treated fairly (8). Then, divide students back into groups and say, "Now, make a list of similarities in all the ideas about discrimination that you have generated or observed or heard" (22). *(Note to reader: Include also similarly related legal, constitutional, and governmental issues. This will also give you a chance to check the interdisciplinary strategy on the checklist.)* Write a list on the board based on the groups' conclusions (6, 14, 17, 27).

3. Tell the students, "Look at the list on the board that we just completed. One idea most represents the problem of discrimination. What is it? Try to guide them toward the idea that all relate to "different treatment of different groups." Then conclude with the question, *"Would a truly spiritual person of good character participate in this such behavior?" Which virtues are lacking* (6)? Ask if the lack of character involved in such discrimination is at all similar to current environmental issues. *(Note to reader: What number would you put here, and how would this question help students understand the concept of discrimination, the importance of environmental activism, and their relationship to good character?)*

4. Homework: Have each student bring to school the following day three paragraphs, one each describing an interview with a family or community member (19). The interviewee can remain anonymous. The questions each student asks are, "Have you ever discriminated against someone? *Which virtues would most likely help people avoid being discriminatory?"*

Instructional Procedures for Day 4

1. Have students share the information from their interviews. Ask them if they or their family members ever experienced discrimination (5, 6, 12, 17, 23). *Tell them that courage, honesty, and humility may be required to share answers. Acknowledge those that obviously show these virtues.*

2. Divide people into their groups and ask them to come up with one way to help reduce discrimination at the school (1). *(Note to reader: Problem-based learning is a most effective way for internalizing association virtues and should be used as often as possible in all subjects.)*

    Help the students identify real-life problems during this session. Have a spokesman from the group write the idea on the board (12, 14). Then bring the class to a consensus about which activity to carry out before the end of the semester (19, 20, 21, 30, possibly 31). Facilitate so the project is realistic. *(Note to reader: Again, if you teach teachers, have your students explain why we chose these numbers from the checklist and how such approaches to learning contribute naturally to character development.)*

3. Give a test to everyone that shows a variety of examples and nonexamples of discrimination from all the areas of study (4) and as they relate to probable situations the students face in their own lives. Tell students to circle only those that are acts of discrimination. *A second and final part of the test asks the students to write one paragraph explaining why having courage can keep people from being discriminating against others.*

Number of Opportunities for Teaching Character Development

I counted nine that I underlined, but the students brought up virtues half a dozen times more. I did not record them in my notes, but I will try to remember them the next time I teach this unit.

Number of Teaching Strategies Used from Checklist

I used 22 of the 31 strategies during the four days that I was able to note and used some repeatedly. I also directly referred to spirituality once.

Teaching Strategies Not Used

I did not use field trips, references to wellness and fitness, music, or kinesthetic intelligence orientations. For wellness, I might have mentioned that people are often prejudiced against others because of their own low self-esteem. Fitness enhances self-esteem, so it may be an aspect of discrimination prevention. If I had had more time to organize it, I think we could have conducting a service-learning experience by working for a day in the inner city, helping at the soup kitchen where mostly minorities use the service.

Closure and Assessment

On the fifth day, hand back the papers. Make sure the students know why they received the grade they did (if you must use grades), and that they know what mistakes they made. Ask the students what they learned from the unit, and how it might help them in their lives.

Personal Reflection

I should have brought some American Indian music to class the day we talked about the Trail of Tears. As for the special project the class is going to do, I think the principal will like it. We can take time during each day for students to create antidiscriminatory posters for the hallway.

I am amazed at how the students saw the need for the virtues when we talked about Andrew Jackson and the Trail of Tears. They were teaching themselves more about virtues and good character than I was teaching.

Some of my students still display prejudice against others. I can't expect a four-day class to have accomplished miracles. However, I have noted that the some did have better behaviors this week than usual. Discussing their cases and building on the work we are doing this semester in subsequent grades will make a big difference by the time they are seniors.

PEDAGOGY AND PROCEDURES CHECKLIST

(Note that the inner skills, the multiple intelligences, and the various teaching strategies are all combined in this checklist. Use chapter 3 for clarification of terms and strategies.)

Teacher's Name   Joe Smith

Subject   Social Studies/U.S. History

Thematic Unit   Discrimination

Grade Level   5

Date Last Modified   June 24, 2000

Directions: Refer to this list to ensure that you use all or most of the approaches one or more times during the unit while creating and implementing your lesson plan. Check which days you used the particular approach.

	Day 1	Day 2	Day 3	Day 4
1. Cooperative learning	X		X	X
2. Field experience				
3. Intrinsic motivational strategy		X		
4. Extrinsic motivational strategy	X		X	
5. Student ownership of subject matter	X			X
6. Critical thinking exercises		X	X	X
7. Intuitive exercises	X			
8. Visualizations	X		X	
9. Dramatizations		X	X	
10. Emotional management opportunity			X	
11. Musical orientation				
12. Logical orientation			X	
13. Spatial orientation				
14. Linguistic orientation			X	
15. Kinesthetic orientation				
16. Interpersonal orientation	X			
17. Intrapersonal orientation	X		X	X
18. Nature orientation				
19. Community involvement				X
20. Multicultural aspect	X		X	X
21. Service-learning activity				X
22. Interdisciplinary connection			X	
23. Dialogue opportunity	X	X	X	X
24. Use of technology	X			
25. Use of humor	X			
26. Reference to wellness/fitness				
27. Peer teaching			X	
28. Mediation				
29. Story-telling	X			
30. Contribution to school environment				X
31. Activism opportunity				X

Notes

1. Marker and Mehlinger, 1992, pp. 830–85.

2. Robert Sternberg's research, published in *Thinking Styles*, reveals that the main reason for upward mobility in most institutions is not excellence or ethics but compliance with the authority figure's way of thinking. This may be especially true in schools, since schools' historic purpose has been to socialize future workers.

3. By saying that social studies is an ideal place for teaching virtues, we do not wish to imply that other courses are not also natural; they are. In fact, if we were to write another book illustrating our approach to character education across the curriculum, we would integrate the content areas, as well. In other words, science, social studies, language arts, math, and physical education all would be intermingled with virtues. We attempt to do this intercurricular integration with our coursework at Oglala Lakota College. We have not done it here because our first goal is to get character education into the existing system as a priority, but most K–12 schools still fragment subject areas.

4. We wish to acknowledge Mike's work in including American Indian issues in his unit on discrimination.

5. Our notes to the reader are excellent teaching aids for readers who are teaching student teachers, and are opportunities for clarification, reflection, and learning for the reader.

Chapter 6

Language Arts: The Art of Sharing Experience

*All effective communication is an experiential
sharing between speaker and listener.*
— Maurice Merleau-Ponty, *The Phenomenology of Perception*

*In indigenous cultures, language has a power all its own,
and to speak it is to enter into an alliance with the vibrations of the universe.*
— F. David Peat, *Blackfoot Physics*

Living Language

Although social studies may seem to be the most natural avenue for studying and developing virtues, literature probably has been the richest resource for teachers over the years. A little research on the web reveals a variety of book lists for character education.[1] However, literature-based character education tends to interpret and freeze experience only in terms of the author's narrative. Students are not likely to internalize virtues from such works unless they make associations with their own experience. Lesson plans work best when the story relates the listeners to one another and to each person's reality.

This experiential sharing is what has made story-telling such a powerful way to teach virtues in American Indian cultures. American Indian stories enhance experience because the language automatically conceptualizes the narrative in terms of comparing recent events to the realm of infinite possibilities. The stories are not frozen events in the past, present or future. Literature-based character education works best when it relates to virtues into a whole, keeping the experience alive so each listener can integrate it into his or her own world.

Don's Story

When I think of communication as a truly sharing experience, I often think of my personal encounter with the "realm of infinite possibilities." Before offering a practical exercise in lesson plan development, I tell my story in the hope it will help clarify this spiritual dimension of the language arts potential.

For 15 years, while working as a professional emergency medical technician, I encountered matters of body, mind, spirit, and language without really understanding their mutuality. Only after my own near-death experience on a kayaking expedition in central Mexico and a rescue out of the canyon by Raramuri Indians did my senses awaken to the realization that they are, in fact, inseparable.[2]

Before this experience my rapport with my patients was technically oriented. I never considered my words' powerful influence on their healing. I was critical of any association with spiritual matters or the "invisible realm" of interconnections that might be at play.

Joe Murdock and I had at least this in common. I did not know him, although he lived in my fire department's jurisdiction. If I had, I would have recognized his cynical, overly rational view of life. Recently divorced and remarried, he had not spoken with his teenage son in a year. He scoffed at his new wife's interest in matters of the heart with an ironclad pragmatism that seemed to fail him in his daily encounters with life. Joe had little faith in his fellow man, less in spiritual matters, and was even losing ground in his work as a stockbroker.

On the afternoon of May 7, 1983, fate set up a first meeting between Joe and me.

"Throckmorton Ridge, respond to a man down at 323 Hawthorne Street," the dispatcher's voice repeated while the alarm continued to sound. I jumped into my turnouts and ran to open the garage door while my captain jumped into the fire engine and started the diesel. Within four minutes we were on the scene. An attractive woman in her 30s, dressed in a nightshirt and barefoot, opened the front door and waved us inside.

"Please hurry. He's downstairs," she said, trying to control her panic. "The basement's flooded. Some of the old plumbing must have busted. Joe was trying to wet vacuum the water. The light bulb went out, and he was changing it and he got shocked and fell and . . . ," she spoke rapidly, trying to give us as much information as possible before we reached her husband.

Joe Murdock was lying on his back in several inches of water. Exposed wires from an old ceiling light fixture indicated that he had been shocked. His heart was pumping, but its rhythm was irregular. My partner relayed the vital signs to the incoming paramedics by radio. Suddenly Joe's body went into a violent spasm, and his eyes rolled back into his head. I pressed on his carotid artery and felt no pulse. Tilting his head back to establish an airway, I placed an oxygen mask on Joe's face and my partner gave him a thump on the chest. Nothing happened and we began two-person CPR.

Before the wild river in remote Mexico tossed me into the underground tunnel, I thought CPR was strictly a mechanical procedure. I could have talked about the weather or a football score while pumping on someone's chest without concern. Now I felt differently. I spoke to Joe continually, telling him what we were doing and encouraging him to help us. I transferred a feeling, also—a feeling that came from deep inside me. It conveyed a sort of camaraderie, a sharing of the experience at hand that seemed to extend back and forward into infinity. Somehow I knew Joe had more life to live, and my responsibility was to make sure he did not forget this. On the river I had learned that death was nothing to fear. Now, suddenly, I understood that fear of death also stifled life's great potential. So I told Joe the worst was over, and he could allow his heart to begin beating again. I thrust the communication into Joe's heart with my hands. I prayed it telepathically into his mind. Then I said it out loud, and my partner looked at me as if I were crazy.

Suddenly Joe opened his eyes and looked into my own. By the time the Mill Valley paramedics loaded him into the ambulance, his heart rate was normal.

Two days later I was back at the station, polishing the wax on our new fire engine, when someone rang the front door bell. It was Joe and his wife.

"Are you one of the guys who came to my house the night before last? I'm the guy who damned near electrocuted himself to death."

"Yes, of course. Please come in. I'm Don Jacobs. My partner went to headquarters this morning but . . ."

"You," he interrupted, "You're the one I wanted to talk to. I mean I wanted to thank both of you, but I know your voice. You were the one who talked to me when I was unconscious aren't you? You, I mean, I think you saved my life and . . ."

His wife interrupted as Joe stumbled for words and his eyes began to fill with tears.

"What Joe is trying to tell you is, well, we think he's alive because of some connection you and he made when his heart was stopped. He remembered everything you said. According to the doctor, it was a miracle that Joe was able to leave the hospital the next day."

Joe had collected his thoughts and emotions and gently took his wife's hand.

"Don, I'm not very good at this, and I guess you guys do this sort of stuff all the time, but, well, I just wanted to thank you."

We looked at one another for what seemed an eternity until another car pulled up the driveway. A young teenage boy got out and joined us.

"Hi, Dad. Hi, Julie. Sorry I'm late. I brought an extra water pack for our hike on Mt. Tam today. Wow, what a cool fire engine. Can I look at it?"

Joe's smile spoke volumes. He looked at me and I nodded.

"Sure, you can climb up inside if you like," I said to the boy. "You guys stop back by after the hike. I'll have some iced tea ready."

As the reunited family worked their way up the trail behind the firehouse, I closed my eyes and said, "Thanks, God, thanks."

In 1997 I returned to Copper Canyon and lived with a 103-year-old Raramuri shaman named Augustine Ramos. He told me that when we are injured or ill one of our souls leaves the body and we don't get better until the soul returns. He said souls need to communicate with other souls to thrive, and that they are reluctant to return to a person who closes off such conversations. He said my own experience on the Rio Urique had taught me this and asked me if I remembered this truth.

I thought of Joe and smiled.

Jessica's Story

Dad holds to the traditional Indian views on language that words have power. He sundances with the traditional Lakota people and has seen the miracles of sundance prayers. I am also learning that words, although they are only the map, not the territory, can become entities in and of themselves in many ways. When I write or speak, I keep this in mind. If my language is good and enters the world, perhaps it will counteract the destruction that seems to be getting so close to us.

This magical aspect of language was made clear to me when I bought a certificate to "fire walk" for my husband, Paul, and me. After building a huge fire and spreading the coals out along a 20-foot runway, our group of average, middle-class people of all ages listened to stories, sang songs, and used word phrases as ceremonies to prepare us for walking barefoot along the red-hot coals.

Everyone in the group managed to walk successfully across the hot coals after several hours of this ultimate practice of the language arts. Then the leader of the event asked Paul and me if we would like to try something. Our confidence in the mysterious forces at work was high, and we agreed. He had us stand several feet apart, facing each other, and placed a four-foot long section of ⅜-inch rebar so that the ends were sticking into the notches just below our throats. We had to push against it slightly to keep it from falling to the ground.

He asked us to concentrate on our love for each other and on the potential of our relationship while we stepped toward each other and into the rigid metal. The metal bent like rubber into a horseshoe shape!

I know this may be a radical example of the power of language, but it is important for us to remember that language can have a significant effect on character development. Literature and communication in all of their forms should be seen as political forces that can shape our perceptions of reality. We teachers should teach communication skills accordingly.

A Learning Exercise

In Indian country, it is usually better for a student to observe something often enough to imagine being able to do it before actually trying to do it. In western culture, students usually are asked to try and learn from failing. You decide for yourself or ask your student teachers to decide if they want to look at more examples (in the subsequent chapters) before trying to write an integrated lesson plan on their own. If you are ready to try, we offer this chapter to walk you through a simple, one-day lesson. Or you may study some more examples in the following chapters first. (Our recommendation is that you finish this chapter so you can be involved more actively in reading the later examples.)

For this exercise we have selected a simple, one-day lesson plan commonly used in language arts. This 50-minute lesson was designed to emphasize students' verbal descriptive and listening skills. We chose it because we thought it did not lend itself to our approach to teaching virtues across the curriculum so we could use it to demonstrate that the approach does indeed work for any existing lesson plan.

Remember, the idea is to:

1. have the intention of teaching a universal virtue while teaching the academic subject
2. by using as many strategies from the Pedagogy and Procedures Checklist as possible,
3. and seeing how the strategy opens the door for a virtue lesson.

This lesson is suitable for fourth to 12th graders. It was presented originally to the Encarta Learning Zone Schoolhouse by Krista Scott, a teacher at Pine Lake Middle School in Issaquah, Washington.[3]

Step One

Fill in the following lesson plan format using the information listed below.

The title is "Creating Vivid Mental Imagery through Descriptive Language." Grade level is fifth grade. Academic subject is Language Arts. Time allowed is 50 minutes. Academic goal is to enhance verbal descriptive skills and listening skills. State standard is, "Student uses listening and observation skills to gain understanding" and "Student communicates ideas clearly and effectively." Character Education goals will surface as you go through the lesson with the intention of teaching the core virtues, checking the Pedagogy and Procedures Checklist for strategies that will stimulate opportunities. Resources and Materials include visual images (the images for this lesson can relate to whatever context you and the students choose that relates to other content areas you are studying); drawing paper; coloring pencils; and a container with numbered slips equal to the number of students in the class. Create your own opening question for the academic focus, then go back after writing the lesson and write in a stimulating question about virtues.

LESSON PLAN FORMAT

Title

Teacher's Name:

Academic Subject:

Character Subject: *(Note to reader: Fill this in* after *you have written the lesson plan because ideas are likely to surface as you go along.)*

Thematic Unit Title:

Grade Level:

Time Allowed:

Opening Questions
Academic:

Character: *(Fill in* after *writing lesson plan narrative.)*

Official Content Standard Addressed

Student Prerequisite Skills and Knowledge
Academic:

Character:

Resources and Materials

Learning Goals
Academic:

Character: *(Fill in* after *writing lesson plan narrative.)*

Specific Objectives
Academic:

Character: *(Fill in* after *you have gone through the exercise once.)*

Step Two

Using the following original procedure for this lesson, write out the "Instructional Procedures" using as many strategies from the Pedagogy and Procedures Checklist as you can. Interject the virtues-related teaching opportunities and underline them. After each step, try to identify what strategies from the Checklist you can use for the specific step in the lesson plan. Then rewrite or add to the procedure using these strategies. As you do this, if you are thinking about the virtues, you will see that chances for teaching the virtue as it relates to the lesson plan procedure will pop into your head. Before beginning, read all seven steps in the original procedure so you have an overview of what the lesson is all about.

1. Have students draw a number from the container and sit in numerically ordered pairs. For example, #1 sits directly facing #2.
2. Have even-numbered students take a piece of drawing paper to their desk.
3. Have odd-numbered students pick an image, making sure not to show it to their partner.
4. As students face each other, the odd-numbered student begins to describe to the even-numbered student what is shown in the picture. Direct the students to be as accurate and complete as possible. Neither person can say or guess the name of the animal or give any verbal clues that help might identify it. The even-numbered student draws on the paper what the odd-numbered student describes.
5. The odd-numbered student may not touch or gesture to the even-numbered student—the student must explain the image through words alone.
6. After the drawing is complete, have the even-numbered student guess what object his or her partner tried to describe. Then have this person look at the original image.
7. Have the pair analyze what was easy and what was hard about the process. Did the odd-numbered student describe the image adequately?

Now, interject and identify strategies from the Pedagogy and Procedures Checklist and create a new narrative that embeds related virtues and/or concepts from the Conceptual Model. After completing this, look at our effort at this exercise. If you are stumped at first, look at our first two examples, then go back and create your own. (Make a copy of the Checklist and the Conceptual Model and have them handy for this exercise.)

Original Lesson Plan's Instructional Procedures

1. Have students draw a number from the container and sit in numerically ordered pairs. For example, #1 sits directly facing #2.

2. Have even-numbered students take a piece of drawing paper to their desk.

3. Have odd-numbered students pick an image, making sure not to show it to their partner.

4. As students face each other, the odd-numbered student begins to describe to the even-numbered student what is shown in the picture. Direct the students to be as accurate and complete as possible. Neither person can say or guess the name of the object or give any verbal clues that help might identify it. The even-numbered student draws on the paper what the odd-numbered student describes.

5. The odd-numbered student may not touch or gesture to the even-numbered student—the student must explain the image through words alone.

6. After the drawing is complete, have the even-numbered student guess at what animal is or her partner tried to describe. Then have the person look at the original image.

7. Have the pair analyze what was easy and what was hard about the process. Did the odd-numbered student describe the image adequately?

Before comparing your new lesson plan with ours, finish yours with the rest of the lesson plan format, continuing to write down the corresponding strategy you chose from the Checklist and the virtue associated with the assignment. Remember to go back and fill in the character goals and objectives.

Homework

Closure and Assessment

Follow-up Activities

Number of Opportunities for Teaching Character Development *(Note to reader: Go back and count how many underlined references to virtues, directly or indirectly, you used.)*

Number of Teaching Strategies Checked on Pedagogy and Procedures Checklist *(Note to reader: Go back to your narrative and count how many strategies you were able to use in this one lesson. Notice that we used [below] 21 of the 31. It seemed the more we used, the easier and more creative we were able to be in thinking of ways to embed virtues.)*

Strategies on Checklist Not Used *(Note to reader: Noting which ones were not used helps with future lessons by helping ensure we do not consistently ignore certain strategies.)*

Personal Reflection *(Note to reader: Although this section refers to reflecting on actual classes taught, you might use it to reflect on how easy or difficult this assignment was.)*

Our Example

Now we will present our effort to do this exercise. Our opening questions are: "What can you learn from today's communication lesson that will help each of you do to have a better relationship with your friends and family?" (academic), and "What does good character have to do with communication that leads to better relationships?" (character).

Instructional Procedures

(Note: The original lesson is in bold type. Our modifications follow.)

1. **Have students draw a number from the container and sit in numerically ordered pairs. For example, #1 sits directly facing #2.** Before each person draws a number, ask them both to close their eyes and imagine creating a partnership that will help both partners get the most from the lesson (1, 2, 5, 7, 8, 16, 27). *Tell the students that if they trust the mysterious forces at work during such concentration (spiritual awareness), their partner may not be the person they hoped it would be, but likely will be the person most likely to contribute to their learning. Ask them to consider how humility and generosity relate to this process. (Note to reader: By simply scanning the Pedagogy and Procedures Checklist, we were able to think of this brief additional focus. For example, when we saw "intuition orientation," we asked ourselves, "How could intuition tie into this lesson?" When we thought of the intuition exercise, imagining how the class would respond to it helped us think of how virtues might relate. Note also how many items it uses and how these lead to the opportunity to refer to the underlined virtue work. For example, just being aware that you have introduced the idea of peer teaching [27] brings generosity into the picture. As the actual lesson unfolds, this concept may also lead to patience or courage [if relationship issues emerge.])*

2. **Have even-numbered students take a piece of drawing paper to their desk.** If the paper is recycled paper, mention this. If it is not, tell the students that you wish it were and that perhaps later a *plan for using recycled paper might be discussed by all (plants seeds for caring and generosity)* (18, 22, and spiritual connection). *(Note to reader: With this brief comment, a nature orientation, an interdisciplinary idea, and a spiritual awareness were all inserted, with future plans for dialogue and activism put in place. The relationship between paper and "nature orientation" on the Checklist is what prompted us to think of mentioning recycling, and this led to planting seeds for caring and generosity. We underlined our comment or reference to these virtues so we could identify it easily later.)*

3. **Have odd-numbered students pick an image, making sure not to show it to their partner.** All the images are illustrations or pictures of animals on the endangered species list (10,18, 22). *Mention that honesty and patience might play into the simple rule of not showing the image to their partner, and that it is up to each of them whether practicing these virtues will lead to a meaningful learning experience.* We thought to make the images animals because we wanted another chance to use spirituality, nature, and ecological sustainability. By doing so we did not take away significantly from the academic goals, we were interdisciplinary in our approach, and we opened doors for teaching virtues.

4. **As students face each other, the odd-numbered student begins to describe to the even-numbered student what is shown in the picture. Direct the students to be as accurate and complete as possible. Neither person can say or guess the name of the animal or give any verbal clues that help might identify it. The even-numbered student draws on the paper what the odd-numbered student describes** (13, 14). *(Note to reader: Can you see why we used these two numbers, which really apply to each step?) Remind students again that it is up to them whether they participate honestly in this process because it will determine how much both partners gain from it (honesty, generosity, respect, and responsibility)* (1, 16, 18, 14, 27).

5. **The odd-numbered student may not touch or gesture to the even-numbered student—the student must explain the image through words alone.** Tell them to notice whether this takes any patience or emotional control. Share the humor that involves noticing how frustrating it may be to avoid using gestures for some, and how it is *an opportunity to practice patience and perhaps even humility.* Also, joke about the possibilities of pictures not looking anything like the one being described (13, 25, 29). *(Reader, can you explain why these three strategies apply and how they helped lead us to talking about patience and humility?)*

6. **After the drawing is complete, have the even-numbered student guess what animal his or her partner tried to describe. Then allow this person to look at the original image.** Allow for healthy humor and laughing about the drawn images (25). *Remind students that not everyone is a great artist (humility) and that it probably took some genuine courage to participate in this lesson. Ask the students to comment on whether or not they thought courage was required and why. (5, 17, 23, 25). (Note to reader: Another advantage of selecting as many teaching strategies as possible is that it gives teachers spontaneous and creative ways to change the way we usually teach, even if in small ways.)*

7. **Have the pair analyze what was easy and what was hard about the process. Did the odd-numbered student describe the image adequately** (1, 6, 12, 23, 27)? What did the students learn about language and communication? About nonverbal aspects of communication? About cooperative aspects of talking and listening? How could different descriptions be improved? Why were some images more accurate than others? *Ask which of the virtues played most into the actual exercise. Then ask which virtues were violated by people who have been responsible for making these animals extinct. (Note to reader: Remember, the goal of character education is to get our students to think about the virtues and their personal value in real life. We are not trying to inculcate virtues or control behavior with this program, but we want to plant seeds and stimulate genuine reflection. This is not just the Indian way, it is the best way to learn.)*

Homework

Use the Internet to research the animal your team selected, and write one page on why this animal is becoming extinct (22, 24). Also identify one thing the class might do to contribute to saving the animal from extinction (31). Finally, ask the students to write one paragraph describing what they learned about communication from the exercise, and one paragraph stating what they learned about practicing virtues.

Closure and Assessment

The homework assignment will serve for both purposes here.

Follow-up Activities

During another class period, students select one or more ideas for saving a selected animal from extinction and do what they can to implement this idea (1, 18, 19, 20, 31). *(Note to reader: Can you see why each of these numbers is used?)*

Number of Opportunities for Teaching Character Development

We were able to teach six virtues (generosity, patience, humility, courage, respect, and spiritual awareness) in each of the seven steps, or seven times.

Number of Teaching Strategies Checked on Pedagogy and Procedures Checklist

We used numbers 1–3, 5–8, 10, 12–14, 16–20, 22–25, 27, 29, and 31 or 23 items out of the total 31. (And this is only for a one-day lesson!) We used several more than once.

Strategies on Checklist Not Used

We did not specifically use any extrinsic motivators (4), dramatizations (9), musical orientation (11), or a kinesthetic one (15). We did no service learning (21), although we might be able to turn the activism activity into this. Opportunities for mediation might have come up in the actual class, but we did not preplan for any here (28). We also did not really contribute specifically to the school environment (30).

Personal Reflection

This section is, of course, for reflecting on an actual class experience. For this exercise, we note that the lesson grew into a meaningful character education opportunity with relatively little extra time or effort.

Checking under day 1 the strategies used provides a useful and easy-to-read log for future reference. As an exercise, go ahead and check the strategies you used when creating your lesson plan.

PEDAGOGY AND PROCEDURES CHECKLIST

(Note that the inner skills, the multiple intelligences,[4] and the various teaching strategies are all combined in this checklist. Use chapter 3 for clarification of terms and strategies.)

Teacher's Name _____

Subject _____

Thematic Unit _____

Grade Level _____

Date Last Modified _____

Directions: Refer to this list to ensure that you use all or most of the approaches one or more times during the unit while creating and implementing your lesson plan. Check which days you used the particular approach.

	Day 1	**Day 2**	**Day 3**	**Day 4**
1. Cooperative learning				
2. Field experience				
3. Intrinsic motivational strategy				
4. Extrinsic motivational strategy				
5. Student ownership of subject matter				
6. Critical thinking exercises				
7. Intuitive exercises				
8. Visualizations				
9. Dramatizations				
10. Emotional management opportunity				
11. Musical orientation				
12. Logical orientation				
13. Spatial orientation				
14. Linguistic orientation				
15. Kinesthetic orientation				
16. Interpersonal orientation				
17. Intrapersonal orientation				
18. Nature orientation				
19. Community involvement				
20. Multicultural aspect				
21. Service-learning activity				
22. Interdisciplinary connection				
23. Dialogue opportunity				
24. Use of technology				
25. Use of humor				
26. Reference to wellness/fitness				
27. Peer teaching				
28. Mediation				
29. Story-telling				
30. Contribution to school environment				
31. Activism opportunity				

LESSON PLAN FORMAT

Title: Junk Mail Persuasion Tactics	Learning Goals	Official Content Standard Addressed
• Academic subject: *Language Arts* • Character subject: *Honesty and generosity with the opportunity to cover more* • Grade level: *9* • Time allowed: *50 minutes × 2 days* • Date last modified: *8/08/00*	Academic: *To increase student awareness of persuasion tactics used in "junk mail" advertising* Character: *To realize the potential for misuse of virtues, to practice generosity*	5. *Students use spoken, written, and visual language to accomplish their own purposes (e.g., for learning, enjoyment, persuasion, and the exchange of information).* 6. *Students apply knowledge of language structure, language conventions, media techniques, and figurative language, to discuss and critique print text.*

Specific Objectives	Resources and Materials
Academic: *Read direct mail advertising critically, identify persuasion techniques, use critical thinking about misleading techniques, neatly label and organize junk mail into a term paper folder.* Character: *To recognize and communicate ways in which virtues are misused, to understand the importance of honesty in sales and marketing, to practice generosity while helping neighbors and by recycling.*	• *Smolowe, Jill. (1992). "Read this!!!!!!," Time, (November 26): 62–70.* • *"Why You Buy: How Ads Persuade," The Learning Seed, 1988.* • *The Bum's Rush (1994), Don Jacobs* • *The Junk Mail Handout* • *Sample Mail and Analysis* • *Bulletin board with examples of each persuasion tactic* • *Student materials: junk mail collected for one month, notebook paper, tape or glue, pen, highlighter, folder*

Student Prerequisite Skills/Knowledge	Opening Questions
Academic: *Be able to define "persuasion"and "marketing"* Character: *Can give examples of honesty and generosity*	Academic: *A letter arrives in the mail addressed to you. You open it and inside you see the word, "Congratulations!" in big letters. You read on about how if you act immediately you will be one of very few people selected to receive a brand new car. There is a phone number to call to claim your prize. What do you do?* Character: *If you called the number you found out that all you have to do to get your new car is attend a presentation about vacation rentals and your name will be put in a raffle. Were any virtues violated in the ad? What virtues might you need to respond properly?*

Lesson Plan Example: Grade Level 9–12

Now that you have had the opportunity to create your first lesson plan using our integrated approach, look at the one below completed by one of our student teachers. This one easily meets the content standards while offering genuine opportunities to address a variety of significant, real-life issues that involve an awareness of virtues. We have left off the part of the lesson plan that asks you to count the strategies used or not used and the number of times virtues were addressed. If you or your student teacher completes this, it will help you to learn the process. Think about or discuss more creative connections with the virtues or better ways to help students internalize them.

Instructional Procedures for Day 1

1. Students have been given a week to collect "junk" mail from friends and family (2). If collected from the neighborhood, students should interview the neighbor to ascertain their opinions about junk mail. Remind students that it sometimes takes *courage* to start a conversation with a person you don't know well (16, 19, 23). Students can offer to destroy address labels to protect privacy (remind them to keep their promise and discuss the importance of *honesty*). Students tell the neighbor that their class is planning on writing a form letter that can be sent directly to companies to stop junk mail, and that a copy of this letter will be given to the neighbor. This is a *generous* gesture to both the neighbor and the environment, since junk mail wastes paper. *Ask the students how generosity comes into play* in this field experience and guide them toward this realization. Students also should encourage their neighbors and family to recycle if they do not already do so (18, 21, 31). *(Note to reader: Notice how nicely this projects meets the content standards, yet affords such an automatic opportunity to study and contextualize the virtues.)*
2. Each piece of mail is mounted on a piece of notebook paper.
3. Have students form groups of three to compare and share mail (1, 16). Have each group present their most ridiculous piece of mail or the wordiest and most complicated (14, 25).
4. Using "The Junk Mail Project" handout as a guide, the students (still in groups of three) analyze the mail and identify the persuasion tactic (6). Each paper is labeled with the persuasion tactic used and points earned (4). *(Note to reader: The students will be extrinsically motivated to identify the persuasion tactics because of the point system, but by working together toward this goal and sharing each other's mail, students have the opportunity to practice generosity. Students who have worked longer and harder to collect mail may have to practice patience with those students who have not collected as much, and students with less mail will be reminded of the* fortitude *it requires to follow through with an assignment.)*
5. Students highlight buzzwords or other words to indicate that the mail meets the assignment requirements. (A sample page is given to each student, and a classroom bulletin board displays examples for each tactic.)
6. At the bottom of the notebook page, students should write one or more sentences about the possible misuse of a virtue in the ad, or when an ad "plays to" or violates a virtue. *Give examples of how issues relating to humility, patience, fortitude, courage, and generosity are associated*, positively or negatively, with the ad. Ask students to name the

most obvious virtue that is used one way or the other. Ask students what the result might be of misusing or taking advantage of virtues on society as a whole.

7. Papers are organized in a term paper folder.

8. All extra mail should be recycled (18). *(Note to reader: Any time an environmental issue comes up you can to discuss the virtues on a larger scale. Here, students can imagine the nationwide environmental impact of junk mail. They may discuss the energy required to distribute the mail or how this may affect future generations.)* (A different aspect of generosity can be addressed.)

9. Homework: Students can finish project at home and perhaps gather more mail.

Instructional Procedures for Day 2

1. Finished projects are passed around the classroom for comparison and discussion (6, 23). Classmates should evaluate each other's work, using Post-it® notes. Constructive criticism, suggestions about virtues, and any other valuable comments should be given by classmates and teacher to provide meaningful feedback to students.

2. Final projects are graded according to designated points (20 points are required for an "A"; students collecting additional points earn extra credit) and student evaluations. *(Note to reader: Although this is a graded assignment, remember that students had the opportunity to share mail with each other, collect additional mail after seeing the requirements, and discuss the virtues with classmates. So all students should earn As. If they don't you have an opportunity to discuss fortitude in relation to completing assignments.)*

3. As a class, compose a general letter to companies that distribute junk mail asking them to take your name off their mailing list. Have a volunteer type the letter and either make copies on a disk or distribute hard copies to students.

4. Homework: Students should mail letter to as many companies as possible. The letter also can be distributed to community members so they can do the same for themselves (19, 31).

THE JUNK MAIL PROJECT

Collect advertising mail from your home for one month. Identify and label examples of persuasion tactics to earn a total of 20 points. Organize pages and folder according to the sample and on the bulletin board. Unless it says "each" next to the point value (#1, #2, and #3 only), you may get credit for each numbered item only once. Each "buzzword" may be used only once for each piece of mail.

1. A buzzword (new, free, save, now, real, homemade, sale, easy, taste, hurry, simply, improved, more, better, better, or an exclamation point, etc.). (1 point each for each piece of mail)

2. An envelope with the words, "urgent," "immediate," or open at once," printed on the face. (2 points each)

3. A promise on the envelope of something "free" inside. Mount the free gift on your paper. (3 points each)

4. A piece of direct mail advertising made to seem "personal" by use of a personal name in a place other than the address. (5 points)

5. A direct mail solicitation with no return address or a very vague return address. (5 points)

6. A sales pitch announcing that something has been "reserved" for you or that you have been selected for a complimentary membership. (5 points)

7. A window envelope with what appears to be a check inside. (7 points)

8. A punch-out circle that has to be placed on an order form. (3 points)

9. A seemingly handwritten address or letter that looks like it is from a friend. (3 points)

10. A direct mail ad in a plain brown envelope that appears to be from some government agency. (7 points)

11. A postcard announcing you have won a prize and merely have to call a telephone number to claim it. (5 points for the postcard; 10 points if you call the number and explain the "catch." Do not call a 1-900 number.)

12. An offer of a free gift for your response. (3 points)

13. A direct mail package containing what looks like a credit card. (10 points)

14. A promise to "save you hundreds of dollars" (or more). (8 points)

15. An envelope mailed bulk rate postage but made to appear like express mail, courier delivered, air express, or a telegram. (8 points)

Thematic Unit on Environmental Issues

Now that you have practiced with a prewritten lesson plan that seemed, on the surface, to have little contextual relationship with using virtues in a constructive way, we suggest you write a four-day, thematic unit on a subject that focuses more on improving the world while teaching language arts. Such interdisciplinary lessons make embedding meaningful virtues into a lesson even easier than the above examples. You can search the Internet for some topic of interest or go to *http://www.teachers.net/lessons/posts/20.html* for a good, free lesson plan on communications and the rain forest entitled, "Exploring the Rain Forest Through Print, Graphics, and Sound."

Remember, when creating thematic units for language arts and character education, use the Pedagogy and Procedures Checklist to enhance the many contexts in which language arts can operate, such as self-concepts or personal reflections on significant influences, cultural customs, futuristic considerations, computer applications, problem solving, environmental concerns, or religion.

Notes

1. For one of many examples, see Amy Braman's list of books for teaching virtues to first and second graders at *www.teachers.net/lessons/posts/1155.html*. She includes a dozen or so books under each of the following categories: respect, honesty, cooperation, perseverance, responsibility, self-discipline, compassion, generosity, acceptance, and friendship. Amy is a school teacher in Vestal, New York, who teaches character education. Her e-mail address is abraman@pronetisp.net.

2. This story is told in its entirety in Jacobs, 1998.

3. See *http://encarta.msn.com/alexandria/templates/lessonfull.asp?page=1700.*

4. We have selected Howard Gardner's multiple intelligences for our checklist because each domain brings up new opportunities to evoke or discuss the virtues. When used with our spiritual and natural orientation, such diverse focuses can enhance character development. However, a danger of latching blindly onto the multiple intelligence framework is in allowing it to support an overly individualistic and anthropocentric view of reality. When this happens, a worldview emerges to support consumerism and ignore our dependence on ecological systems. For example, a musical orientation in American Indian culture is a means to develop and perpetuate a process of life-enhancing relationships. Too often, we use multiple intelligences strictly as a way to elicit individualistic aptitudes without regard to the cultural and natural systems that surround an individual's life. For a thorough discussion of this potential problem, see Bowers, 2000.

Chapter 7

Science and Virtue: Partnership for the Future

Will you ever begin to understand the meaning of the soil beneath your very feet?
From a grain of sand to a great mountain, all is sacred.
— Peter Blue Cloud, Mohawk, in Nabokov, *Native American Testimony*

How we organize and study the physical world
should be based on concern for others and sharing the
world by creating an accommodating environment.
— Chongyam Trungap, *Sacred Path of the Warrior*

The Nature of Science

Quantum physics shows how reality is altered to some degree when we interact with it, even if we do no more than observe. American Indians have long understood this phenomenon. From such understanding has come an exceptional belief in prayer and a profound respect for individual viewpoints. On the surface, the latter may seem to be a *relativist* position, but it is not. It is a *relational* position. How different people see the fire depends on their relationship to it. Such a position is, in fact, more absolute than relative. The absoluteness, however, is about relationships that are in the process of change.

American Indian philosophy also holds that mutuality, reciprocity, and goodness are inherent in absolute, natural laws that apply to all the interconnections of the universe. From this perspective, science is about the process of interrelationships that are so comprehensive that they include generosity, fortitude, honesty, courage, etc. Thus our goal as science teachers should be to ensure that these virtues are not ignored so that teaching connects students to the bigger picture rather than separates then from it.

The English language makes it difficult, though not impossible, to make such connections. It relies too much on single answers that are subject/noun/category-oriented. This can cause us to lose sight of the process orientation that science can remind us exists in the world. For example, the name Black Elk in the Lakota language conveys the idea of seeing the silhouette of the elk at sunset or sunrise. Such an interpretation describes various relationships in the process of change, as opposed to categories that relate only to the color black or the species elk. Similarly, describing a tree in most indigenous languages brings into play seasons, wind conditions, types of animals currently living in the particular tree, etc., whereas in English the object is simply *tree*.

Our usual western approach to describing reality also makes it more difficult to understand the spiritual dimension of scientific inquiry. Recall that our definition of spirituality is about our connections to all things in the seen and unseen realms. Respecting the invisible world calls for recognition of mystery as an aspect of our universe, rather than being "supernatural" or above nature. The latter concept "comes from the modern assumption that the natural world is determinate and mechanical."[1] Once we as teachers and as students accept nature as including human interactions, the true nature of science shows itself. By weaving spirituality and virtues into the study of science, it not only becomes a more exciting endeavor, but it also points us all toward more beneficial applications of knowledge.

In one of her lesson plans, Oglala Lakota College science professor Misty Brave has a wonderful unit about the scientific method. In it she talks about the role of virtues in scientific inquiry.

> The Ikce Wicasa (common man) are taught the values of respect, wisdom, generosity and courage at young ages. They determine the strength of the people. These four values provide a backbone for the Lakota Nation.
>
> Remember that scientists are like us too. They have the courage to finish their work and accept the challenges of other scientists. Scientists are generous with their knowledge and will write articles or make displays of their findings. They respect the wisdom of fellow scientists.
>
> Using the scientific method helps you find a way to use your Lakota values.

Lesson Plan Example, Grade Level 3–5

Since in our view ecological sustainability is the most vital of all scientific concerns, we obviously think this subject should be at the root of most if not all science instruction. We realize it might be difficult for teachers always to choose a science project that directly deals with environmental issues. For example, a lesson about teaching the difference between frequency and amplitude is not likely to tie directly to environmental issues. However, if we can embed virtues into such a subject, perhaps we can do this as well with ecological awareness. (Hmmm, maybe this will be our next book.) In any case, for this sample unit we have chosen water, and any investigation into water ultimately should relate to a concern about water quality. We also have elected to use "interdisciplinary connections" from the Pedagogy Procedures Checklist by combining the science lesson with math, language arts, and social studies.

Instructional Procedures for Day 1

1. *Ask the opening questions and give student groups time to come up with some preliminary answers amongst themselves* (1, 3, 5, 16). Walk around the room to ensure they are discussing this and give suggestions to guide their discussions. Afterward, ask students to keep their initial conclusions in mind or write them down for later reference (17). *(Note to reader: Asking how the virtues might relate to a subject and giving students the opportunity to discuss among themselves without the stress of reporting to the teacher is always an effective way to teach virtues.)*
2. Then, as a class, students will list on the board various uses of water (6, 12, 23). Relate uses to the water cycle (12), ensuring each person knows the cycle and the two elements that make a water molecule.
3. Have students estimate how much water they use in a day and for what purposes. *Since it will be obvious to students at this point that excessive use of water is not something to be proud of, mention that answering this question may bring into play a need for courage, honesty, and humility. Briefly explain why.* See if there are any differences among various cultures or socioeconomic groups. For example, do affluent white families wash cars more often or water the lawn more often (20). *By using the multicultural strategy, an excellent opportunity arises to teach students about how class or cul-*

LESSON PLAN FORMAT

Title: Water	Learning Goals	Official Content Standard Addressed
• Academic subject: *Science, social studies, math, language arts* • Character subject: *Generosity, courage humility, honesty, fortitude* • Grade level: *5* • Time allowed: *Four days* • Date last modified: *8-3-00*	Academic: Science: *Students will understand some significant causes of and solutions to water pollution.* Social Studies: *Students will become aware of some social, historical, and political aspects of water pollution.* Math: *Students will be able to measure water amounts.* Language Arts: *Students will write a poem about water,* Physical Education: *Students will learn at least one advantage of exercising in the water.* Character: *Students will gain an awareness of the relationship between solving or preventing water pollution and a variety of the core universal virtues.*	*This unit touches on at least one standard objective in each subject area.*

Specific Objectives	Resources and Materials
Academic: 1. *Name various uses of water, causes and consequences of pollution, and preventive or curative measures.* 2. *Name social reasons and conflicts relating to above.* 3. *Name various measurement units for water.* 4. *Write a poem honoring water.* Character: 1. *Identify which virtues are violated by water pollution issues.* 2. *Identify which virtues are needed to solve problem.* 3. *Demonstrate and reflect on generosity in a water-related project.* 4. *Gain respect for water.* 5. *Demonstrate courage and fortitude by trying something different and sticking with a project through its conclusion.*	*Jell-O mix (6 oz.)* *See-through plastic cups* *Cooking oil* *Cooktop stove and pot* *Soda bottle* *Sponges* *Soil, syrup, salt, paper, soap* *Phosphate test kit* *Microscope*

Student Prerequisite Skills/Knowledge	Opening Questions
Academic: *Ability to follow directions* Character: *Can give basic definitions of the six core virtues*	Academic: *When you drink water how do you know if it is making you healthy or making you ill?* Character: *Is there a relationship between clean water in your community or environment and any of the virtues?*

ture can influence environmental issues that affect us all. (Note to reader: Without mentioning the word, this will be a lesson in humility.) Then ask students to return to their groups and determine how they can reduce this amount by 25 percent (12, 22). *(Note to student teacher: Why is #22 checked?)*

4. If anyone mentions swimming (lead them toward this use of water, if necessary) discuss exercise advantages of water (13, 22, 23). Ask students to close their eyes and visualize swimming in a clean pool of lake water and feel their muscles and lungs working (26). For those who cannot swim, have them imagine running in shallow water. *Now have them imagine being in chlorinated water or polluted water* (3, 8). *(Note to reader: We underline this because this may contribute indirectly to the motivation that leads to practicing virtues. We used visualization and interdisciplinary subject matter to bring in some "intrinsic motivation" regarding the importance of clean water. To practice courage or fortitude or patience, such motivation is critical.)*

5. Homework: Have students measure all the water they use that evening and report to class the next day the exact amounts using both U.S. and metric measurement units.

Instructional Procedures for Day 2

1. Hand out plastic cups, Jell-O, etc., and have students label their cups A or B. Have them put one tablespoon of oil in cup A. Then make the Jell-O and refrigerate it for next day. Ask the students to guess which cup they will want to eat tomorrow and why (15).

2. Have students cut a fish out of a sponge, attach a line and weight to it, and put the fish inside an empty plastic soda bottle. Fill the bottle three-quarters full with water. Tell a story about Freddy the Fish (29) and have the students add one of the pollutants, whichever one seems to fit (5), as the story unfolds and describes different pollutants humans put in Freddy's water. *(Anything that makes connections like this plants the spirituality seeds.)*

3. Use a filtration system to try and remove the pollutants from the water bottle each child polluted (15). Provide the students with sand, coffee filters, cotton, cheesecloth, and funnels. Ask them to work in groups (1) to see which filtration system removes which pollutants best. *Remind them that some patience will be needed to do these experiments and ask them to reflect on whether this is true, and if so, how patience helped them.*

4. Have them squeeze the water out of the sponge fish and compare that water to the water they cleaned. Then ask students to illustrate the food chain that includes fish (6).

5. Homework: Have students write about how the polluted water affects life via the food chain. Have them bring a milk carton size container of water to school the next day that some creature might drink. This can be their own drinking water, water from a pond, a birdbath, etc. (2, 5).

Instructional Procedures for Day 3

1. Hand out the Jell-O and ask the students to eat whichever cup they prefer. Play scary music in the background for effect (9, 11, 5, 25). (Most will not eat the one with oil in it.) Ask them why they ate the one they did.

2. Divide students into groups of two and have them begin testing their water samples for odor, clarity, phosphates, pH, and bacteria using the water-testing kits. Go over results of the tests and discuss what each conclusion might indicate (1, 6, 4, 15, 16, 27). *(Note to reader: Why is "extrinsic motivational strategy" involved here? How does it lead to the possible teaching or practicing of generosity that follows?)* For example, bad odor could indicate algae or sewage pollution. Chlorine odor could indicate processing by a treatment plant. Poor clarity could indicate silt in the water. Phosphates could indicate fertilizers, etc. *Ask students to think of a way people could help others by knowing this information. (Guide them toward ways to use this information to help ensure that others are not getting sick from their water, even if they themselves do not use it.) (generosity).*

3. Homework: Give students a take-home exam that asks them to define limnology and list the physical, chemical, and biological parameters that relate to the study of water. *Tell them this assignment will take some fortitude and patience since they will have to find their own resources (textbooks, dictionary, computer, parents, etc.) to complete it.*

Instructional Procedures for Day 4

1. Take the class to a pond (2, 18). Have them draw pictures of all the creatures they see there (13).
2. Ask them if they think the pond is polluted and to explain their answers (6).
3. Hang the pictures on the wall the next day.
4. Homework: Have the students write letters to selected officials about some known body of polluted water (31). *Have them write a second page explaining what virtues come into play when writing such a letter (6). (Note to reader: If you have been teaching the virtues in this way for some time, the students likely will come up with a variety of associations between courage, patience, generosity, and honesty and this assignment. If not, guide them with questions about possible repercussions and problems that such activism can create.)*

Number of Opportunities for Teaching Character Development

Nine different opportunities (the underlined sentences).

Number of Strategies Checked on Pedagogical Checklist

We used 1–6, 9, 11–13, 15–18, 20, 22, 25–27, 29, and 31, or 21 strategies.

Strategies on Checklist Not Used

We did not use 7,8, 10, 14, 19, 21, 23, 24, 28, or 30. *(Note to student teacher: Can you go back and use each of these strategies in the instructional procedures by adding your own insertions? What new opportunities for teaching virtues arise from these?)*

Personal Reflection

By combining the various subjects, students seemed to appreciate how their own knowledge base applied to the water unit, and I think this motivated them to participate more fully. I feel they learned the required academic standards for science and they better understand the role of virtues in cleaning up our environment.

Notes

1. David Abram makes this statement on page 8 of his 1996 book, *The Spell of the Sensuous*, when talking about the power of medicine men to heal and the misinterpretations of anthropologists. His book ponders the violent disconnection of the body from the natural world that is prevalent in nonindigenous cultures.

Chapter 8

Body, Mind, and Spirit

Long ago we felt the land under our feet and it was good.
We ran everywhere. We stayed healthy.
Now we no longer run on the earth and we are sick in body and spirit.
— a Lakota elder, spoken at a community meeting, 1994

To a friend that we love
Like the sun up above,
Who helped us get ready for living.
We'll work to be healthy,
Instead of just wealthy,
And remember there's good
In just giving.
— a community tribute inscribed on a statue of Reddie Rabbit,
in Jacobs' *Happy Exercise*

Sportsmanship and Fitness

Education standards for teaching physical education generally identify the social and personal responsibility associated with participation in physical activity. It should be a no-brainer to embed the virtues into such courses if the intention to do so is present. Competition especially affords numerous opportunities to practice courage, fortitude, patience, humility, honesty, and generosity. Unfortunately, too many coaches and teachers ignore such opportunities for teaching virtues. As a result, more and more immoral and unethical events cloud the world of amateur and professional sports, and many youth emerge from schools worse for their physical education experience. (A notable exception in the world of professional sports is Los Angeles basketball coach Phil Jackson, who not only incorporates serious references to moral and spiritual conduct in his training sessions, but also specifically uses Lakota spiritual teachings with his players.)

Thus, with committed intentionality, you should find it very easy to use our approach when teaching a variety of sports. Though not as obvious, it is also simple to include the virtues when teaching fitness-related subjects. This is good to know because we think that physical education should be at least as much about proper fitness knowledge as it is about games and sports.

The University of South Carolina's brochure for its annual "Wellness 2001" conference begins, "Health and wellness issues are vital to success in the academic environment." Of course, we all know that a healthy body and mind are mutually beneficial. Fitness also breeds confidence and a healthy self-concept, and these traits restrain ego defense mechanisms that tend to stifle character development. Moral development theorists may think that people do not practice higher-order virtues until late in life, but we wonder what conclusions they would have reached if they had studied only fit, happy, healthy people. Both the Greeks and the American Indians have had much to say about the connection among body, mind, and spirit, and we offer a lesson on exercise in this section that shows how easily children can make connections between virtues and health-related topics.

SAMPLE LESSON PLAN, GRADE LEVEL 1

Title: Developing an Exercise Plan	Learning Goals	Official Content Standard Addressed
• Academic subject: *Physical education* • Character subject: *Character subject fortitude, courage, patience, honesty, humility, generosity* • Grade levels: *1–2* • Time allowed: *50 minutes × 3 days* • Date last modified: *7-3-00*	Academic: *To realize and understand the importance of exercise, develop a realistic exercise plan, understand the role of warm-up and cool down, aerobic and anaerobic exercise* Character: *To realize the role of virtues in developing and maintaining physical fitness, to practice virtues in play and sport*	*Programs (1992) from the National Association for Sport and Physical Education (NASPE); draft of the Michigan Department of Education's Physical Education: Content Standards and Benchmarks (1996).* *Uses a variety of basic and advanced movement forms, uses movement concepts and principles in development of motor skills, understands the benefits and costs associated with participation in physical activity, understands how to monitor and maintain a health-enhancing level of physical fitness, understands the social and personal responsibility associated with participation in physical activity.*
Specific Objectives Academic: *To define exercise, identify various types of exercise, to understand the importance of exercise for life-long well being, understand the benefit of warming up and cooling down, know the difference between aerobic and muscle-building exercise (realizing the importance of both), understand the relationship between a good diet and a good exercise plan* Character: *To become aware of the role of virtues in communication and learning and practicing components of exercise*		**Resources and Materials** • *Cooked and uncooked spaghetti noodles* • *Digital or Polaroid camera* • *Mat for stretching* • *Balls, jump ropes, or other sports equipment* • *Tape deck or CD player for music (and various fast and slow music selections)* • *Poster board and crayons or markers*
Student Prerequisite Skills/Knowledge Academic: *None* Character: *Can give examples of courage, fortitude, patience, humility, generosity*	**Opening Questions** Academic: *Your best friend's family just invited you to spend a week camping with them. They plan on fishing, swimming, hiking, and playing. You are sure you will have the time of your life. The campsite is 12 miles from where you park the car. Are you up for it?* Character: *You decide that you will go on vacation with your friend. Are you in shape? You must exercise every day to prepare for the long hike. You have been exercising each morning for one week, but this morning you were so tired you forgot to get up early and go for a walk. Will you exercise after school instead? Does it take perseverance to stick to your plan?*	

Instructional Procedures for Day 1

1. Ask students to form groups of two and help each other complete the following statement: "I think exercise is_____." Tell students that this is how we will come up with a class definition of exercise. Record responses and then combine them to create one definition (1, 5, 23). Remind students that it is *courageous* to express one's opinion honestly about exercise because it is a sensitive issue for many. *(Note: Simply by using a dialogue strategy, you give students an opportunity to reflect on the virtues that come into play when communicating, such as honesty, humility, patience and courage. But by reminding them of the virtues and bringing this relationship between dialogue and the virtues to consciousness, students begin to identify and internalize the virtues.)*

2. Have students give examples of exercises they do. Record responses on the board. (Use graphics to illustrate the words if prereaders don't understand them.) While listing, separate aerobic exercises and muscle-building ones into two columns and ask students if they can tell the difference between the two columns. Sample responses: "Those are slow and those are fast." "Those make you breathe hard and those make your muscles hurt." Students can role-play and show examples of different types of exercise. *This provides an opportunity to discuss courage and humility by reminding students that performing exercises in front of a group sometimes requires these virtues* (9, 15). Students should be reminded to practice self-control when offering input (10). During the discussion, mention other sports and types of exercise that students are not familiar with, especially those popular in other counties or those used by disabled persons, elderly, etc. (20). *(Note to reader: Remember, planting seeds for* character *is often a subtle endeavor. When young children simply learn about other cultures or about disabled people, the slightest reference to a virtue like humility can go a long way. For example, "Maybe you can run fast, but someone in a wheelchair can be equally fit.)* Encourage students to offer examples of things that animals do to exercise (18). *(Note to reader: Any time we have a chance to show similarities between humans and animals, we move away from the arrogance that allows us to destroy them, thus teaching humility and perhaps generosity.)*

3. Have students sit quietly and still for two minutes and explain that you are conducting an experiment. Tell them the experiment will be fun. Discuss the virtue of patience and its importance in this situation. This is also a great opportunity for talking about emotional self-control at a time when students are not being defensive about bad behavior. *(Note to reader: I did not plan on discussing patience here originally, but it seemed to be a teachable moment for it. All it required was intentionality.)* Discreetly, take a photo (24) of the class during these two minutes of resting.

4. Tell the students that soon they will hear some music and when it comes on they are to stand up and move. They can dance, jump, run, spin, hop, etc., and when the music ends they are to stop and face the front of the room (11, 15). Some students may be embarrassed to participate and should be reminded that it is understood that *courage* and *humility* might be needed here. Tell the students that it is okay to look silly while they are exercising (25). If some students begin to tire, ask them if they know the difference between getting physically tired and just giving up (*fortitude*).

5. When you stop the music, be prepared to snap a photo of the kids (the students probably will be smiling).

6. Show the photos to the class (perhaps on an overhead computer) (24) and ask for comments on the difference between before and after. Lead a class discussion about the way exercising makes you feel (23).

7. Homework: Have students find out from a family member or neighbor what he or she does for exercise and why (19).

8. This information can be presented orally, in written format, or in a drawing (13, 14).

Instructional Procedures for Day 2

1. Before students arrive, list the benefits of the various exercises that were named by the children. The list should include things that students discussed at the end of the period the day before. When students arrive, have them present their homework about what parents and neighbors thought about exercise (demonstrations are appropriate) and add benefits to the board as they come up (14, 15, 19). *(Note to reader: This community involvement assignment will set the stage for a later chance to teach generosity.)*

2. Explain that since class members feel it is important to exercise the class will create an exercise plan, but that first they need to determine what a good exercise plan consists of (5).

3. Lead the class in various types of exercises (each one should work different body parts) (15). This can be done while playing "Simon Says," which presents an opportunity to discuss *patience* and *honesty* (since Simon Says requires participants to be patient and critical when deciding whether to perform a particular task and honest in whether or not they made a mistake). Balls, jump ropes, etc., can be used here.

4. Start off slowly with easy exercises and stretching; explain that this part is called the warm-up (to be discussed further later).

5. After each individual exercise, ask students to determine what part of the body is being exercised. Encourage discussion, especially in cases where one exercise can work many body parts (23).

6. Explain that it is important to exercise every part of the body. All the body parts are connected, so that if one part doesn't get exercised it could affect the entire body. Discuss the connectedness of the body and how it is similar to the connectedness of the class members and of the world. *(Note to reader: By making a metaphor of the interconnections of the body with more universal interconnections, we have incorporated spirituality in this lesson.)*

7. End slowly and cool down (walking, stretching, breathing deeply).

8. Ask students if they know why it is important to warm up and cool down. Have students relax (they should be at a resting heart rate) and visualize (8) what it feels like to run around the block ten times just after waking up. Play fast music (11). Tell students to notice whether it is easy or hard to pay attention to how their hearts feel, listen to their breathing, and feel their legs (8). In pairs, have students describe the feelings (1, 23). Remind students to practice *patience* when listening to one another and to let their partner complete a thought before interrupting. *Ask what other virtues come into play when describing a private visualization to someone. Ask the children questions to help them understand, such as, Does it sometimes take courage to share your own special views? Do you feel like you were being generous when you offered*

your ideas to help someone else learn something? Were you truthful about your visualization? Did you think your visualization was better than your partner's and if so, is this good (humility)? (Note to reader: It is important not to always tell the students what virtues they should be practicing. If they can come up with them on their own, they are more likely to adopt the virtue as their own. With this age group you will have to guide them toward possible answers to the questions.)

9. Have students visualize the situation again, this time describing first waking up slowly, getting dressed in a leisurely fashion, eating a healthy breakfast; stretching the arms, legs, back, neck, ankles, wrists, waist, etc., walking around the block once (slow music should be played here), jogging around once, and finally running. Ask them to notice again if it is easy or hard, to pay attention to how their hearts feel, to listen to their breathing, and to feel their legs. Have students pair off again and describe this different experience (8, 23). Have volunteers share their ideas with the class.

10. Discuss the importance of warming up. Ask if it takes any of the virtues we have discussed to keep from going full tilt into a sport or exercise session without proper warm-up *(lead toward role of patience)*. *(Note to reader: The visualizations can be led in such a way as to bring in examples of impatience or patience relating to an activity.)* Demonstrate with cooked and uncooked spaghetti noodles. Explain to students that the cooked noodles are like muscles that have been through a warm-up. These muscles have been stretched so they are ready to bend and move easily. Show students how easily they bend and move. Then show the uncooked noodles. Explain that they are stiff and are like muscles that have not been warmed up. Show how the noodles break when pressure is applied. When you work muscles hard without a warm-up you may strain them and injury may occur. *(Thus there are consequences to not having patience.)*

11. Explain that it is equally important to cool down and test this (2). Have students do 20 jumping jacks, then sit down and feel their heartbeats. Ask them to notice how they feel.

12. Next, have students do 20 jumping jacks, then slowly walk around the room twice without talking and feel their heartbeats. *Have volunteers describe the difference and ask if the virtue of patience applies here, as well—*e.g., what if they wanted to stop and sit down right away because they felt tired.

Instructional Procedures for Day 3

1. In groups of four, have students discuss all the important parts of a good exercise program (things that have been discussed in class and other ideas that come to mind) (1, 23). Explain that you will be walking around the room to be sure that all students are participating and remind students to remain aware of how *courage, patience, and generosity can play a role in how the talking goes* (4). Write down interesting comments you hear to share with class later. (They might relate idea of sharing to generosity and its value.)

2. Bring the class together to discuss their ideas. Be sure all students know that it is important to warm up and cool down, that both aerobic and muscle-building exercises must be done, and that all body parts must be exercised (although not always on the same day). Share some comments made earlier.

3. If students have not brought it up yet, be sure to discuss the importance of diet in relation to exercise (22). Explain that it does not make sense to make your body healthy by exercising, but then to feed it junk food with chemicals. *Ask if it is easy to avoid eating bad foods and if it is hard to eat only good foods. Ask them what virtue is required to have this kind of discipline (fortitude).* Remind students about what they learned in a previous nutrition unit or implement such a unit here. Also discuss how eating habits of various animals are related to their health and what would happen if they were not fit or if they ate bad foods or foods that are poisoned with pesticides (18). *(Note to reader: This plants seeds for future activism [31].)*

4. Have students return to groups to create a week-long exercise program. This program should provide specific details such as time limits and number of repetitions. The program should be presented on a poster to be hung on the wall. Photocopy the posters so that each group member can take one home (4).

5. Homework: Students implement their programs (2). For extra credit they can include a family member or neighbor who does not exercise currently (19, 21). *(Note to reader: If students do something to help a neighbor, you have introduced them early to the idea of service learning. Make sure their accomplishment is discussed to deepen the meaningfulness of their efforts.)* Be sure to discuss how fortitude relates to sticking with the program and how generosity relates to sharing it with others. Students might tell their new exercise partner that they know how much courage it takes even to start an exercise program. Encourage students to share their knowledge of the importance of practicing the virtues.

Student Teacher/Reader Critique

1. What strategies in this lesson most encouraged teachable moments for character development?
2. Which strategies that were not used would you have used, and how would you have tied them to a virtue?
3. Are there any parts of this lesson plan that might not be a good fit for this age level? Why? If so, how would you change the lesson plan?
4. How many strategies from the Pedagogy and Procedures Checklist were used? How many opportunities for teaching a virtue?
5. Which of the virtues taught, do you think will have the greatest impact on the students?

Note

1. This has been republished by the authors as a coloring book that teaches K–2 graders about virtues and healthy lifestyle habits. See *www.teachingvirtues.net* for ordering information.

Chapter 9

Mathematics and the Invisible Realm

It is not good to take the People out of the equation.
— Lakota elder ("people" includes all creatures,
not just humans), from a community meeting

We must question the basic soundness of . . . education . . . that is divorced
From the limitations and qualifications of organic existence.
— Louis Mumford, *Technics and the Nature of Man*

Sacred Numbers

Many teachers have been led to think that mathematics is the least likely of subjects for integrating virtues into coursework. As you will see, character education has no such boundaries. Perhaps this is because we can use math as a way to face the unknown, using all the virtues we need for such heroism. In math we can comprehend the invisible realm just enough to test our character. Also, within this mystery there seems to be something a little sacred about numbers and their relationships.

American Indians seem to recognize this sense of sacredness in numbers. The cave-dwelling Raramuri Indians of Mexico still know the laws of probability.[1] Like many native peoples who remember the old ways, they can compute the odds of various outcomes in ways that acknowledge the metaphysics of the cosmos. With this skill they gamble joyfully, but they have not forgotten the power of the trickster, so the gambling does not deter them from a good path. Many American Indians remember that there is a sacred connection between equilibrium and numbers, as with the number four and the seven directions.[2] Modern physicists who use math to explain why airplanes fly and apples fall see this connection, as well.

Although our average math students may be a long way from seeing math as sacred, when we teach math in concert with character, this subject can take on a new meaning. Imagine math and character as partners. You might be saying to yourself, "If I can teach character development in a math class, I can do it anywhere!" Actually, math classes offer fertile soil for learning virtues. If teachers help students understand and embrace patience, courage, and fortitude in math class, they may be able to use these virtues to learn mathematics better. It is the lack of these traits that often prevents students from sticking with confusing math concepts long enough to grasp them, or at least keeps them from being willing to enter into the unknown.

The National Council of Teachers of Mathematics published *Curriculum and Evaluation Standards for School Mathematics*. Standard 7, for kindergarten through grade four, focuses on the concepts of whole number operations and states: One essential component of what it means to understand an operation is recognizing conditions in real-world situations that indicate that the operation would be useful in those situations.[3]

Unfortunately, most math teachers rarely use real-world situations to teach math. They spend most of their time with paper and pencil arithmetic. (Since teaching virtues also works best when real-world applications are considered, such a method does not lend itself to our partnership between math and character particularly well.) To move toward real-world problem solving, teachers must provide time for students to grapple with real-life problems on their own. Such work requires a shift in students' attitudes that embrace the virtues. According to Marilyn Burns,[4] students who learn math with real life in mind must develop certain characteristics. These characteristics are listed below. Following each one, we relate a corresponding virtue to it. Note how relevant the virtues are to the characteristics identified by Burns. (We underline the virtues here to help accustom you to this practice that we recommend for your lesson plans.)

- **Students must have an interest in finding solutions to problems.** Genuine interest in a subject increases when we are courageous enough to venture into unfamiliar territory; when we show sufficient humility to admit we know little about the subject and are interested in knowing more; if we have enough fortitude to study something long enough to become intrigued by it; if we have patience to listen long enough to know whether we are interested; and when generosity motivates us to be interested in something outside of ourselves.
- **They need sufficient confidence to try various strategies.** This calls for *courage* and *fortitude*.
- **People learning math must be willing to risk being wrong at times.** Such willingness is enhanced with the development of *courage* and *humility*. (Consider story of Jamie Escalante of East Los Angeles's Garfield High School where, in 1982, he motivated poor Hispanic students to shine in calculus by constantly telling his students all they needed was *ganas* [courage].)
- **They also will be more likely to excel if they are able to accept the frustration that comes from not knowing.** This may be impossible without some degree of *humility* and *patience*.
- **Related to handling frustrations that come from not knowing is the willingness to persevere when solutions are not immediate.** This willingness improves as students practice *fortitude* and *patience*.
- **Math students must develop an understanding of the difference between not knowing the answer and not having found it yet.** Again, *patience* is required.

Thus, teaching virtues in the math class has four benefits. The virtues help with the math; the math helps with teaching virtues; the intention to combine math and virtues using the Pedagogy and Procedures Checklist pushes us to follow national guidelines for using independent and cooperative problem-solving activities to learn math; and the math exercises are more likely to focus on global, community, or ecological issues that make math meaningful and put the virtues into real-life contexts. (For example, if you are discussing exponential growth, why not use related social implications such as population growth for illustrations, and then discuss the virtues associated with such issues?)

Math typically is viewed as a no-nonsense system of black and white formulas and equations. Many teachers, students, and administrators feel uncomfortable considering anything beyond equations and formulas. Equations without relations, however, make it difficult to embed virtue awareness. For example, it is common for a math teacher to teach that $5(a + b) = 5a + 5b$. Not many chances to talk about generosity so far. But if the problem is presented as follows, more teaching strategies from the Checklist and, hence, more virtues can enter the equation (no pun intended):

"Class, the Koati bear is extinct in the wild. Two are in captivity at the New York Zoo. This number will be "a." Three are in captivity at the London Zoo. This number will be "b." If breeding would result in five times the current number of animals in captivity and we want to release 20 animals into the wild, how many would remain in the zoo?"

Students can come up with the answer any way they want according to our philosophy, but someone is guaranteed to wind up using the formula we want to teach—i.e., 5 (a + b) = 5a + 5b. Or $5 \times 2 + 5 \times 3 = 25$. (Thus the answer is that 20 animals can be released, leaving five in the zoos.)

Why would a real-life approach make it easier to teach virtues? First, approaching the subject in this way allows the teacher to use a variety of approaches from the Pedagogy and Procedures Checklist. These pedagogies are about relationships of all kinds—relationships between self and others, self and self, self and nature, etc. Virtues exist in the context of relationships, so the more strategies we use, the more opportunities we have to teach virtues. In this case, the subject matter itself is about relationships involving other creatures, extinction issues, etc. This affords even more chances to talk about the role of courage, fortitude, generosity, and other virtues.

For Student Teachers

If you are a teacher trainer or student teacher, these sample lessons are great resources that offer many opportunities for constructive exercises and homework. Students can reflect on how they would use their own ideas to join content and character. They can look for virtue insertions that seem too contrived or that are more about behavior than moral development, and they can discuss why they believe this is so. Student teachers can create, add, subtract, or modify the use of the various pedagogical strategies, and they can evaluate their success after practical applications of their own lesson plans based on these examples.

Sample Lesson Plan, Grade Level 12

Our point in offering these illustrations is to help you understand how to embed virtues into content. Many of the comments and examples we offer in this chapter are important for other subjects, as well. Do not worry if some of the math jargon is foreign. Our goal here is to show how virtues can be taught without interrupting content. (In this first day's lesson, we use a strategy similar to what we used in the practice exercise for the language arts chapter.)

If this is your first day with this class, an introduction something like this one might set the stage for the rest of the term:

> To be successful in this class, you must participate fully. You will not learn to do math just by watching me do it. Math is not a spectator sport and neither is learning. If a concept seems too challenging, be patient and give yourself some time for it to sink in. If you are stuck on a difficult problem, don't give up, practice fortitude instead. If something is confusing, be courageous and ask questions of your classmates and me. If you understand a topic, and a fellow student is struggling, be gen-

LESSON PLAN: MATH IN THE GARDEN

Title: Math in the Garden	Learning Goals	Official Content Standard Addressed
• Academic subject: *Mathematics–Geometry* • Character subject: *Fortitude, courage, patience, honesty, humility, generosity* • Grade levels: *10–12* • Time allowed: *50 minutes × 4–5 days* • Date last modified: *4-2-00*	Academic: *To demonstrate ability to communicate mathematically, create fractals, recognize geometric series; to be aware of mathematics in nature, understand tiling of the plane, recognizing symmetry, and using properties of polygons to build the optimal-shaped garden* Character: *To realize the role of virtues in communication, problem solving and living in harmony with nature as demonstrated through expressed understanding and observed behaviors*	*Analyze characteristics and properties of two- and three-dimensional geometric shapes and develop mathematical arguments about geometric relationships; apply transformations and use symmetry to analyze mathematical situations; use visualization, spatial reasoning, and geometric modeling to solve problems. (NCTM, 2000)*

Specific Objectives

Academic:
To describe in detail shapes a fractal and a geometric series; attempt to tile the plane with various polygons; to build fractals with polygons; create tilings with the Fibonacci sequence; optimize area with a given perimeter; recognize mathematical properties in nature and build a mathematically efficient garden (actual garden optional)

Character:
To practice fortitude while tiling the plane, predicting and calculating area and perimeter, and caring for the environment; understand the role of and demonstrate courage while taking a risk based on someone else's direction and in actions related to protecting the environment; show patience and understand its importance while following directions and manipulating tiles; contemplate and practice honesty during direction activity; taste humility if and when one's product is far different from anticipated; and express and enjoy generosity while sharing with others and caring for the environment

Resources and Materials

• *10 sets (for class of 30) of photocopied diagram*
• *pattern blocks*
• *crayons or colored pencils*
• *white drawing paper*
• *centimeter-wide strips of paper*
• *rulers*
• *scissors*
• *gardening books*
• *slides of examples of math in nature (optional)*
• *materials to build a garden (optional)*
• The Magic of Mathematics *by Theoni Pappas*

Student Prerequisite Skills/Knowledge

Academic:
Knowledge of properties of polygons, perimeter and area, basic geometric sequences, and symmetry

Character:
Ability to define and offer examples of fortitude, courage, honesty, humility, and generosity

Opening Questions

Academic:
What math do you need to build a garden? What math will nature create in the garden?

Character:
What virtues are needed to build a garden? What virtues are needed to do mathematics?

erous and help out. Be honest at all times; don't try to cheat your way through, because that will only hurt you in the long run. Let me know what I can do to help you achieve your goals. Remember, we are all in this together, and no one is better than anyone else. Be humble in knowing that we are each only a small part of this great universe (a universe that can be described using mathematics).

Instructional Procedures for Day One

1. Divide students into groups of three (1). Give each person one of three envelopes containing photocopies of the directions (see figures A, B, and C below). Each student needs a blank sheet of paper and something to write with. Desks must be arranged so that the three group members have their backs to each other and are away from the other groups.

2. Have one student from each group open the envelope and follow the instructions. The other students follow the oral directions given by this student. Each student should have approximately ten minutes to describe the image contained in the envelope (13, 14, 16). *(Note to reader: By starting out using several of the multiple intelligences, we are setting the stage for the kind of relationships that involve the various virtues, if you as teacher are watching for them.)*

3. Remind students they are not to look at anyone else's work. Explain that it will be very tempting to do this and *that this is a great opportunity to practice honesty. (Note to reader: In this situation, since no grading or testing is involved, discussing honesty will not be seen in behavioral terms. This gives the students a chance to truly consider integrity as it relates to "doing what is right," rather than complying with a teacher's mandate about cheating.)*

4. Explain that students should use critical thinking, intuition and visualization to help give and receive the images (6, 7, 8). Instruct them to use humor (25) if possible and have fun with it. Ask later how they used each of these approaches. *(Note to reader: Once these aspects of the conceptual model and Checklist are familiar to students, it becomes easier to move from them into the virtues. For example, critical thinking often brings up courage, humor can lead to humility, and intuition can stimulate generosity.)*

5. *In between turns, ask students what virtues came into play during the exercise, especially when their picture did not come out right. How do patience, honesty, and humility make this assignment easier to do?* What real-life situations can you think of where such virtues associated with similar challenges would have resulted in a healthier outcome, less frustration and more happiness (10)? *(Note to reader: Realize here that you have not strayed from the math objectives. Once students understand how patience, honesty, and humility relate to the assignment, they will find future assignments easier and will begin to make connections in other areas of their lives.)*

6. After students have accomplished the task, ask them to volunteer their observations about the images themselves and how they were communicated (23). Ask if the method of delivery helped to get others to recognize properties of the shape, fractal, and sequence (27).

7. Briefly lecture about bubbles and hexagons (when a sphere is tangent to other spheres that are tangent to each other, a hexagon is formed), fractals and the Fibonacci sequence. The Internet is a good resource for examples (24). Talk about Fibonacci and

how he came to discover the sequence (29). *Ask the class what virtues he must have had to have accomplished what he did after describing a little of his personal history. (Note to reader: Telling stories about someone's true life often brings in opportunities to teach virtues. This association makes math more meaningful, and it also may inspire a future mathematician.)*

8. For the night's homework, have students bring in examples of hexagons, fractals, or the Fibonacci sequence as it is found in nature. If they use a natural object, have them take a picture or make a drawing if it can't be brought to class. *If they remove a natural object, like a branch from a tree or a wild stone, suggest that they ask the object's permission to remove it, express gratitude for it, and leave food or hair in its place as a sign of respect. During the next class, ask students who did this to describe how they felt doing this ritual. Tie this to ideas about interconnectedness, respect, and generosity in a brief dialogue with the class* (2, 5, 18). This may seem weird to high school students, but simply remind them that it is not a religious ceremony of any kind; it is just one way of showing respect to our fellow planet-mates. *(Note to reader: One reviewer said we should take this idea out of the book. He thought it would be an explosive issue. You and your students should decide if the concern has value or not.)*

Figure A

Directions: Describe this image to your partner so that he or she can replicate it. You may not use numbers (for example, don't say, "Draw three lines or draw one circle or add those two numbers"). Use any other mathematical terms that you know to help your partners draw the image.

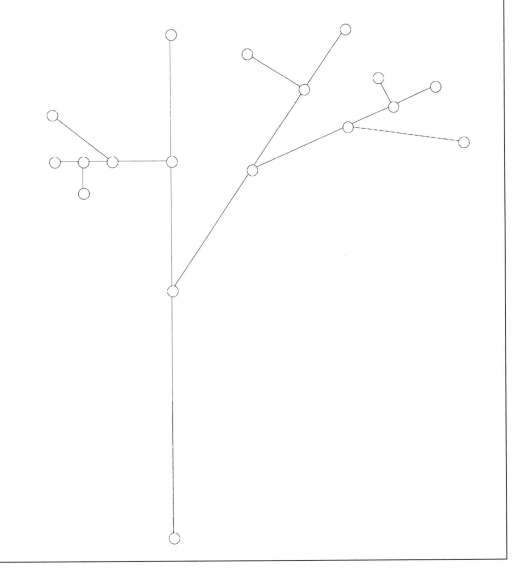

Figure B

Directions: Describe this image to your partner so that he or she can replicate it. You may not use numbers (for example, don't say, "Draw three lines or draw one circle or add those two numbers"). Use any other mathematical terms that you know to help your partners draw the image.

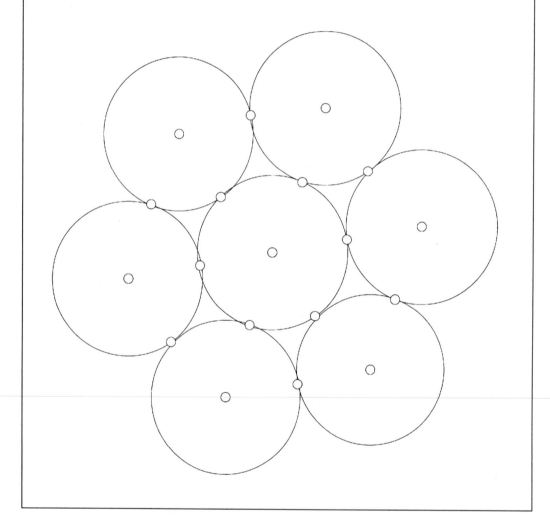

Figure C

Directions: Describe this sequence to your partner so that he or she can replicate it. You may not say a particular number. Use any other mathematical terms that you know to help your partners draw the sequence.

0, 1, 1, 2, 3, 5, 8, 13, 21, 34, 55, 89, 144, 233, 377, 610, 987, 1597, 2584, 4181

Instructional Procedures for Day 2

1. Have students share the examples of math in nature they brought from home (18). First remind students about how *it takes courage and humility to present in front of a class.* (Ask someone to explain why this is.) *(Note to reader: Overcoming performance anxiety is a common thread in most classes that can be related to one aspect of courage. Each time you use such an opportunity, give it a different twist that relates to the students' personal situations.) Instruct presenters to show their object and ask the class if they can find the math in it (5).*

2. Pass out pattern blocks. If there are not enough, mention that this is a good time to use the virtue of generosity *and share with someone.* Students should work in the same groups of three as yesterday (1). Try to divide the blocks evenly so that each group has about the same number of each shape. *(Note to reader: Teaching generosity when everything is going well is much better than bringing up the subject when students are being thoughtless or greedy.)*

3. Allow students to play with the blocks to become familiar with them (15). Ask them to identify things in their neighborhood that have the same shape (2, 5).

4. Assign the following three tasks. Each of the three group members is responsible for one of the three assignments. If one person finishes early he or she should help one of the other two or do task C for fun (*generosity*) (5, 27).

   a. "Fractal" each of the pattern blocks—i.e., use squares to make a larger square, triangles to make a larger triangle, etc. Let students determine on their own that you cannot make a hexagon from smaller hexagons. Once they realize this, see if they can make hexagons using a combination of other polygons. *Ask those who try if fortitude was required. (Note to reader: Students' responses make take one or two minutes if you do not get off track here. But just this small amount of time to bring the concept of fortitude to conscious awareness will go a long way toward teaching the virtue.)*

   b. Tile the plane or a piece of paper using the pattern blocks. Ask if all the shapes tile the plane. Ask if the students can make a shape that won't tile the plane (5).

   c. Make a design with any or all of the pattern blocks using the Fibonacci sequence in some way. Copy the design onto a sheet of drawing paper using various colors.

5. Have students present their findings to the class (27).

6. Show a microscopic picture of a leaf cell and how similar shapes appear in nature (18). Take a moment for everyone to ponder why such shapes exist so often when we look at nature under a microscope. *(Note to reader: Opportunities like these that show relatedness are teaching spirituality in the classroom, but we are sure no one will take you to court over it.)*

7. Discuss tiling the plane in more depth and show examples of M. C. Escher's work. Ask questions about when and how nature tiles the plane and show how honeybees do it every day (18). Does this offer proof of how we are all related?

8. Discuss the virtues used (or not used that should have been) during this activity.

9. Homework: Measure the perimeter and area of a square, a triangle, and a hexagon. Students may use any method. For example, if they do not know the formula to calculate the area of a hexagon, they can measure the area using beans.

Instructional Procedures for Day 3

1. Discuss how the mathematical ideas explored on days 1 and 2 relate to a home garden (23).
2. Ask students why they think honeybees use hexagons to build their honeycombs.

   Pose the following question and give students (while still in groups) the class period to (a) solve the problem and (b) to write an essay, create a poster, or give a power point presentation (24) about their solution. Ask: "What shape is ideal for a fenced-in garden?" and assign the class to create such a garden on paper (any form of media may be used for this) (1, 2, 5, 8, 12, 13, 15, 18, 23, 24). *(Note to reader: Can you explain why each of these pedagogies is checked? Can you explain why using so many of them opens doors for teaching character that would not be open if only lecture or workbooks were used? For example, as students give their answers based on their field experiences, how many will differ in their ability to actually have a garden, and what social issues that involve virtues might arise?)*

   Make manipulatives available (strips of paper to simulate wood, etc.). There is no wrong answer here, although a good model uses a hexagon since this maximizes area using the fewest materials, or a rectangular model shows the benefit for rows inside.

Instructional Procedures for Day 4

1. Have students present their garden design and give each other constructive criticism (6) about any aspect, from space efficiency to planting certain plants next to others if some students happen to know about gardening. *Use this opportunity to teach humility in accepting constructive criticism and honesty in giving it. (Note to reader: Again, remember that our goal is to contextualize activities in the classroom and in the larger community in such a way as to make virtues relevant.)*
2. Give students time to research types of plants to put in the garden by having them use the Internet and available garden books (18, 24). *Show how such research can call for patience and fortitude. Also talk about issues that relate to worldwide starvation, abundance and scarcity, and economic habits that stifle good nutrition. (Note to reader: Is it likely these subjects will relate to any of the virtues?)*
3. Tell the students to choose plants where they can identify the math ideas that were studied during the previous days. (Help them understand this connection.)
4. After determining how much room each plant requires, ask students to design a planting diagram of their garden with their group (5).
5. Discuss the benefits of having a garden. Encourage students to plant a garden with the cooperation of neighbors and family members (19). *Ask what generous act they could do as a class, a smaller group, or an individual that relates to their knowledge about building gardens, sharing garden space, sharing food from the gardens, etc.* Brainstorm ideas about making a garden that is earth-friendly and affordable—i.e., using recyclable materials (19, 21, 31). *If time permits, discuss which virtues are required to make a commitment to recycling.*
6. If possible, get other classes involved in planting a school garden or distributing vegetables to classes (30). Have students vote for their favorite design and make copies of it to give as gifts to other classes and to teachers and administrators. *This provides another opportunity to practice generosity.*

PEDAGOGY AND PROCEDURES CHECKLIST

Title _____ **Math in the Garden** _____

Academic Subject ____ **Mathematics - Geometry** _____

Character Subject ____ **fortitude, courage, patience, honesty, humility, generosity** ____

Directions: Refer to this list to ensure that you use all or most of the approaches one or more times during the unit while creating and implementing your lesson plan. Check which days you used the particular approach.

	Day 1	**Day 2**	**Day 3**	**Day 4**
1. Cooperative learning				
2. Field experience				
3. Intrinsic motivational strategy				
4. Extrinsic motivational strategy				
5. Student ownership of subject matter				
6. Critical thinking exercises				
7. Intuitive exercises				
8. Visualizations				
9. Dramatizations				
10. Emotional management opportunity				
11. Musical orientation				
12. Logical orientation				
13. Spatial orientation				
14. Linguistic orientation				
15. Kinesthetic orientation				
16. Interpersonal orientation				
17. Intrapersonal orientation				
18. Nature orientation				
19. Community involvement				
20. Multicultural aspect				
21. Service-learning activity				
22. Interdisciplinary connection				
23. Dialogue opportunity				
24. Use of technology				
25. Use of humor				
26. Reference to wellness/fitness				
27. Peer teaching				
28. Mediation				
29. Story-telling				
30. Contribution to school environment				
31. Activism opportunity				

(Note to reader: use this form for the previous unit by noting which strategies were used on which days without using the numbers in the Lesson Plan.)

7. Homework: Find a community member or organization interested in creating a garden or create a visual presentation of math in nature to share with elementary school students (18, 19). *It might take courage and/or fortitude to call around to find someone interested in building a garden.*

Closure and Assessment

I ask the class to offer the two most important character education concepts they realized, learned, associated with, or practiced during the week, and the two times where such concepts were most lacking in both classroom activities and more global contexts that were discussed. In the same manner, I then share my own observation notes of students during the week and how the virtues and the concepts of respect, wisdom, and spirituality (interconnectedness of all things) played out. I grade the individual and group homework assignments on mathematic reasoning skills as they relate to the subjects we covered. The students will be asked to write an entry in their math/character journal.

Personal Reflections

Luis was frustrated that he did not understand what Jan was describing. He finally turned around to look at her picture. I think a private conference to talk with him about emotional control and honesty would help him focus more on these things.

The students asked me so many good questions about tiling and fractals, they caught me off guard. Next time I will be better prepared to answer them.

The students really enjoyed the M. C. Escher work I brought in. Next time maybe I'll show an Escher documentary or arrange a field trip to the Escher museum.

The activity was worthwhile, but no one actually helped build a real garden. I need to think of ways to make this more likely to happen with the parents and community. Perhaps I will get permission to create a school garden. We could bring food to the inner city, and this would be the service-learning opportunity I have been looking for.

After studying my "Pedagogy and Procedures Checklist," I realized that I did not sufficiently use #3, intrinsic motivational strategies; #9, dramatizations; #11, musical orientation; #20, multicultural aspects; #22, interdisciplinary connections (though I did use some writing across the curriculum when I asked them to write an essay); #29, story-telling; #26 reference to wellness (gosh, this would have been a natural with a discussion about the health benefits of organic gardening); or an opportunity for the class to participate more fully in consciousness activism (31). I will keep these omissions in mind for the next unit.

LESSON PLAN: BUYING A CAR

Title: Buying a Car	**Learning Goals**	**Official Content Standard Addressed**
• Academic subject: *Mathematics* • Character subject: *Fortitude, courage, patience, honesty, humility, generosity* • Grade levels: *7–9* • Time allowed: *50 minutes × 4–5 days* • Date last modified: *5-14-00*	Academic: *To demonstrate use of arithmetic computations, graphs, numerical projections and comparisons and problem solving* Character: *To realize the role of virtues in planning and saving*	*Understand numbers, ways of representing numbers, relationships among numbers, and number systems; understand meanings of operations and how they relate to one another; compute fluently and make reasonable estimates; understand patterns, relations, and functions; analyze change in various contexts; use mathematical models to represent and understand quantitative relationships; develop and evaluate inferences and predictions that are based on data (NCTM 2000)*

Specific Objectives	**Resources and Materials**
Academic: *To predict how much money can be saved in five years as determined by specific variables. Assessment will be based on performance, use of problem-solving processes, working effectively as a team member, justifying decisions based on mathematical support* Character: *To describe how a commitment to following a specific car-buying plan can test courage, humility, honesty, perseverance, patience, and generosity, and to practice these virtues during the unit. Assessment will be based on expression of virtues during process and justifying decisions based on the virtues identified*	• *Internet access* • *newspaper ads for used and new cars* • *consumer magazines* • *debt-to-income ratio formula*

Student Prerequisite Skills/Knowledge	**Opening Questions**
Academic: *Basic reference and research skills, knowledge of functions, Internet skills* Character: *Ability to offer adequate definitions for virtues*	Academic: *What can you do to ensure you can buy an adequate car for yourself when you are a senior in high school?* Character: *What virtues would come into play when planning to buy your first car and are they important to the process?*

Sample Lesson 2, Grade Level 6–8

For our grade level 6–8 four-day thematic unit, we have chosen the title, "Buying a Car." We think this topic is relevant to many young people in this age group, especially 8th graders. We also believe that education about finances is lacking in our schools almost as much as character education. By the end of the four days, students will have learned how math skills, virtues, money, and automobile purchasing are inextricably connected, as are most things in life. Such relevancies in choosing thematic units make character education across the curriculum meaningful.

This approach is almost like reading children stories that have metaphors and morals we want them to learn. We take every opportunity to engage the youngsters with voice inflection, questions, recent life experiences, etc., to make sure they get the point. We want our lesson plans to feel this way. American Indian parents used stories to teach children necessary skills and virtues, but they continually referred back to the stories during life experiences and teachings. This is how the mathematics involved with buying a car can be seen, as well.

Instructional Procedures for Day 1

1. Form students in groups of three to five (1, 16).
2. Each group draws monthly salary figures from a box (20). They have exactly 60 months to save money for a car. Their salary will increase by 10 percent each year. They can use all of it for their car, or they can give a portion of their monthly salary to their family or to someone who may have a greater need. *This plants a seed for the concept of generosity. (Note to reader: Indirect teaching is always more powerful than direct teaching. By not specifically using the word* generosity *sometimes, but still describing a generous act, you may be more effective in teaching generosity.)* Remind them that if they choose to give some of the money away they should be sure they have enough for dependable transportation. They must determine how much money they will have at the end of the five years, and they have three options for saving: a shoebox; a savings account at 3 percent interest annually; or an index fund account at 10 percent interest annually. *(Would such a plans call for fortitude or patience?) (Note to reader: This time you may need to mention the virtues because the correlation is not as obvious.)*
3. They can use the money saved in five years either as a down payment if they can qualify for a loan, or to pay cash for the automobile. Since no one can know what kind of cars will be here in five years or how much they will cost, assume that cars currently available will be the only ones available in five years. Have them imagine what kind of cars might be around in five years and discuss their ideas briefly (8).
4. Give the class 30 minutes to figure how much money they plan on having in 60 months for a car and/or for giving away, entertainment, clothing, etc. (12).
5. Play classical music with stringed instruments (16) during this time, and make the rounds to each table to facilitate student work. Some groups may work faster than others so ask groups that are ready to determine how big a loan they would qualify for based on their down payment and a constant salary (realistic for a high school student). Give the Web site for a loan payment calculator and debt to income ratio *(http://www.webfoot.com/cgi-bin/loan.pl)* and monthly payment table from

http://www.financenter.com or similar Web site (24). Discuss good versus bad credit with individuals or the entire class.

6. With the music still playing, have groups settle down and guide everyone in two visualization exercises. The first has them driving their ideal dream car down a country road (8). Refer to the beauty of the nature along the road (18). Have them stop for an animal crossing the road. Describe the animal (18). Suggest that they notice how much gasoline per mile they are consuming. This is a good opportunity to introduce $d = rt$ and formula transformation (i.e., $r = d/t$).

7. Now, bring everyone back to the here and now, reminding them how good they feel. Begin the second visualization by asking them to imagine driving down the same country road in a less expensive, second choice car. Tell them they have this choice because they gave some of their money to a family in their community whose house had burned down and had no insurance to replace lost clothing. Have them notice how equally beautiful the drive is and how good they feel about having helped the family. Have them notice also that this car uses less gasoline (perhaps, since less expensive cars tend to get better gas mileage). *(This is helping to instill the concept of generosity. Ask the class how it does.)* Bring everyone back to the present feeling good in every way.

8. For their homework assignment, ask the students to come to class the next day with a recommendation from someone in their family of which car to buy. Also, ask them to find out if anyone in their community has had a tragedy or other circumstance causing that person or family to have a special need for financial help (19). This is *another opportunity to consider the responsible action necessary to implement generosity. (Note to reader: It seems that car ownership is often contrary to concepts of patience, generosity, and humility so we are not surprised to find that generosity is the virtue that keeps popping up. Remember, these opportunities arise naturally from the assignment; we are not basing the assignment on them.)* Finally, ask each student to call three car dealers of any car and ask a salesperson for the price of that car. If they ask why you want to know, be honest and say it's for a class project. Ask if it will take *courage* to make these calls and see the next day if and why it did. Students are to report the next day on these homework assignments. Send permission forms home for a field trip to some car dealers, along with a letter asking parents to help with calls if necessary.

Instructional Procedures for Day 2

1. Open with a story (29) about a young man who was offered a great job after school during his junior year in high school. But he needed a car to get to work, because there was no public transportation from his house to the job site. He figured he could afford a car payment, but he could not afford the monthly parking fees in the city near his place of employment. He thought and thought about this problem. What do you think he did (6)? He learned there was a nice free parking area just outside the city limits, about 1.5 miles from his job. He decided to drive to this place about 40 minutes early and walk to work. Besides saving the high parking fees, what else did he accomplish by having to walk to and from his car? Talk about physical fitness, *but also about proper humility and the role it would have in doing this* (26). Is *fortitude* required to do this, also? Why? *(Note to reader: Physical fitness is a natural subject to raise when talking about cars. Why is this?)*

(a) Encourage dialogue about the homework assignment (23). Ask if different dealers gave different prices for the same car. Discuss whether the concept of *honesty* relates to the differences (which there are, especially if students did the research on-line) (24). If it is obvious that some students did not do the assignment, encourage honesty about this fact. Be clear that there will be consequences (4) for not doing homework and state what they are. Reinforce the fact that being honest about it ultimately is the best policy. Explain why. *(Honesty and courage can be discussed here.)* If there were serious discrepancies, have the class construct a letter (14, 22) that you write on the blackboard to the dealer(s) with the highest prices, complaining about the lack of integrity of charging more for the same car (31). Have the class decide if they actually want to send the letter and arrange for this to be done by having a volunteer write it and everyone sign it (1, 5). *Does it take courage to take responsible action against wrongdoing?* Have a few students role-play what one of them would say to a dealer (9) who sold him or her a car that cost $1,000 more than a dealer down the street was charging for the same car. Teach emotional control in this role-play (10).

2. Have the students form into their groups again. Today they are to decide what car they want to buy (3, 5) and if they can afford to buy it (5). Make available the periodicals, *Car and Driver*, *Consumer Reports*, etc. Also refer them to *http://www.kbb.com* for blue book prices. Advise students to consider how the car performs more than how it looks. Tell a personal anecdote or other humorous story about ugly cars. Personal story: I had a 1969 Valiant that had been in an accident. We were constantly pulled over by police just because it was so dented. When I would ask the officer why he pulled me over, he would say, "I don't know yet. Something must be illegal." Nothing was ever wrong, and it was a most dependable car. (25, 29).

(b) There is bound to be some disagreement in the groups about which car to buy. If so, this is a great *opportunity for patience, humility, and generosity training*. Ask one of the groups to argue its points in a mediation demonstration with the goal of reaching an agreement on what action to take next in the decision process (6). If no serious disagreement exists, ask members of a group to pretend to disagree (9, 28). Discuss gas cost (depending on miles per gallon) versus use (commuting, cruising, utility only, etc.).

3. For homework, each student has to calculate how much money he or she would have in 60 months with each of four options: save all the money in a shoebox; save all the money at 3 percent; save all the money at 10 percent; save 80 percent of the money at 10 percent, having given 20 percent away to charity. Assuming there is no debt, have students use the debt to income ratio to determine how much they can borrow for a car using all their money as a down payment.

Instructional Procedures for Day 3

1. Ask a leader from one of the groups to go to the board and replicate the homework assignment with the help of his or her teammates. Make a game out of this by saying that whichever team has all the correct mathematical answers with clear explanations (4), that team decides which car dealer the class will visit on the field trip the following day. *If there is a clear winner, take the opportunity to teach humility as an aspect of com-*

petitive exercises. Each team has the opportunity to go to the board. If more than one team has perfect answers, the decision is made either by collaboration or by drawing numbers. Collect homework assignments and grade them.

2. Once it is clear that everyone knows how to figure how much money he or she will have to spend, how much can be borrowed, and which car to buy, have the group members take turns explaining their decisions about why they chose a particular car (6). Have *students relate to virtues in explaining reasons* (prompt if necessary) and note the quality of reasons in your assessment log.

3. The group that won the "no math errors/clear explanation" game or won by chance chooses someone to make an appointment with a car dealership for a class visit to hear a sales pitch for the chosen car (16). (The teacher should back up this call also to ensure the appointment is confirmed, explaining the reason for the trip.)

Instructional Procedures for Day 4

1. Class goes to two or three dealerships (2) with researched price quotations for the car and listens to the sales pitch with *respect (talk about issues of respect that relate to how the salesperson and the students act).* Perhaps a salesperson can bring the car to the school parking lot. The salesperson explains costs relating to operation, insurance, and fuel, and details about loans on new and used cars.

2. Discuss differences in price quotes, sales pitches, and possible issues relating to ethics.

Closure and Assessment

Ask class what they learned about numerical projections and the need for math skills. If grades are required, individual student participation should have been noted throughout the four days. Day 3 homework assignments are graded. Also ask the class to share how the six virtues were involved throughout the unit, and how they would be important in a real-world process of planning for and buying a car. Tie what the class has learned to the concepts of respect and wisdom. Give an exam on the math concepts, or have groups turn in an essay reflecting their efforts during the unit. Ask them to write one way they actually displayed one of the virtues and one way they did not when they could have. These can be put into a student portfolio on character that can be used in the next grade levels.

Follow-up Activities and Homework

Ask students to do one generous act relating to automobiles over the weekend. Perhaps this means washing someone's car or helping someone shop for a good bargain *(generosity).* Be prepared to discuss during the following class period how it felt to do this before beginning another thematic unit. Ask them also to note if and how this act called for any mathematical knowledge.

PEDAGOGY AND PROCEDURES CHECKLIST

Thematic Unit Title ___Buying a Car___

Academic Subject ___Mathematics___

Character Subject ___generosity, courage, patience, fortitude, humility, honesty___

Grade Level ___7 - 9___

Directions: Refer to this list to ensure that you use all or most of the approaches one or more times during the unit while creating and implementing your lesson plan. Check which days you used the particular approach.

	Day 1	Day 2	Day 3	Day 4
1. Cooperative learning	X	X	X	X
2. Field experience				X
3. Intrinsic motivational strategy		X		
4. Extrinsic motivational strategy		X	X	
5. Student ownership of subject matter	X			X
6. Critical thinking exercises		X		
7. Intuitive exercises				X
8. Visualizations	X			
9. Dramatizations			X	
10. Emotional management opportunity		X		
11. Musical orientation	X			
12. Logical orientation	X			
13. Spatial orientation				
14. Linguistic orientation		X		
15. Kinesthetic orientation				
16. Interpersonal orientation			X	
17. Intrapersonal orientation	X	X	X	X
18. Nature orientation	X			
19. Community involvement	X			X
20. Multicultural aspect	X			
21. Service-learning activity				X
22. Interdisciplinary connection		X		
23. Dialogue opportunity		X		
24. Use of technology	X	X		
25. Use of humor		X		
26. Reference to wellness/fitness			X	
27. Peer teaching	X			
28. Mediation		X		
29. Story-telling	X			
30. Contribution to school environment				
31. Activism opportunity		X		

Personal Reflection

I'm afraid the car salesman was a little upset with our not buying a car. Next time I will explain we were just practicing. I'll discuss with the class whether we were not being respectful by not being clearer about our goals. Samuel was especially excited about the project, but I allowed him to focus too much on what kind of a car to get and did not push him enough to understand the math lesson. I need more opportunities for him to learn humility also.

I need a funnier story about cars. I'll be on the lookout. Maybe we will listen to a recording of the Car Talk radio program.

I feel the students and I have done more than just plant seeds for generosity, fortitude, honesty, and courage. During the next unit I will focus more on humility and patience.

Our class did not find time to contribute to the school environment. If I make this a six-day unit, perhaps we could teach the fifth or even eighth graders how to plan for buying a car.

As usual, I am not involving the students in nature often enough. Maybe a field trip to a place where we can ride horses in the wilderness would put automobile buying into a perspective that would make having an expensive automobile less important. I think such an experience in nature for these kids add to their courage to be less materialistic, would add to the patience with regard to social pressures to conform, and who knows what other virtues might be stimulated when they have more chances to restore their bond with the earth.

(Note to reader: An eight-page lesson plan for a four-day unit is about the right amount of preparation for a new program. Our teachers at Oglala Lakota College are finding that referencing the Pedagogy and Procedures Checklist and inserting teachable moments for virtues and underlining helps them remember and use the ingredients for good education.)

Sample Lesson 3, Grade Level 3–5

Humility is a difficult concept to convey to children in grade levels below 3–5. When it is partnered with truthfulness, children tend to understand its value. In this lesson, we do something a little different. Rather than have our character education goals emerge in the process of teaching content that is not normally identified with virtues, we have intentionally structured an assignment to include both. Some teachers will find this easier to do initially. Of course, ways of teaching both content and virtue will still emerge automatically if you are looking for them and if you are using the Pedagogy and Procedures Checklist and the Conceptual Model.But starting with an obvious connection may be helpful for both teachers and students, especially at the lower grade levels.

Before a unit like this can work, an earlier class session is required in which the terms have been discussed thoroughly.

Instructional Procedures for Day 1

LESSON PLAN: PERCENTAGES

Title: Percentages	Learning Goals	Official Content Standard Addressed
• Academic subject: *Mathematics* • Character subject: *Honesty, humility* • Grade levels: *3–5* • Time allowed: *50 minutes × 4 days* • Date last modified: *5-14-00*	Academic: *To help students extend their understanding of how to reason with percents* Character: *To increase awareness about practicing honesty and humility*	*Understand numbers, ways of representing numbers, relationships among numbers, and number systems; understand meanings of operations and how they relate to one another; compute fluently and make reasonable estimates; understand patterns, relations, and functions, analyze change in various contexts; use mathematical models to represent and understand quantitative relationships; develop and evaluate inferences and predictions that are based on data (NCTM 2000)*
Specific Objectives Academic: *To demonstrate engagement in dialogue, activities, and question answering as they relate to the problems and contexts presented* Character: *To understand of the advantages and disadvantages of showing honesty and humility*		**Resources and Materials** • *grocery receipts from home* • *Monopoly money* • *a menu from a restaurant* • *newspaper ads containing percents* • The Bum's Rush *by Don Jacobs*
Student Prerequisite Skills/Knowledge Academic: *Understanding of percents; ability to convert to and from percentages to find the percent of a number* Character: *Can define and give examples of honesty and humility*	**Opening Questions** Academic: *Mr. Perfect says he is right 100 percent of the time. Do you think he is bragging?* Character: *When is bragging an OK thing do to? When is humility and honesty not happening during bragging?*	

1. Have the students engage in dialogue (16, 23) about the opening question for 20 minutes. Once they seem to understand that the question has many shades of color to it and cannot be answered definitively, ask them to form into groups of 4 (using playing cards for random selection) (1, 27). Their assignment is to estimate *(a) what percentage of the day they are completely honest, and (b) how often they do or do not practice humility, also expressed in percentages.* Letter should be sent home requesting volunteers for field trip and including permission slips.

2. Homework: Look for articles or advertisements in the newspaper in which percents are used (22). Each group chooses one person to present to the class. In the presentation the next day, the groups explain the meaning of the percents and the *possibility for dishonesty associated with how the author used percents or how they could be dishonestly interpreted and used by the readers* (6). Ask students to make sure their parents have read the letters inviting them to join us at the store. Make sure you have a signed permission slip from each student. Give class time for them to begin this work if possible.

Instructional Procedures for Day 2

1. In their groups, have the students order dinners based on the menus students bring to class and the ones I have provided. Ask them to determine the total cost of the meal and decide what percent tip they will give to the waiter. Have the group role-play and act out being out to dinner and discussing how much the tip should be and who should pay it (9). *They must explain their reasoning in terms of honesty and humility. (This will involve why people give tips, characteristics of the service, bragging or showing off, how much money people actually can afford to spend, honest feelings about the meal and service, etc.)* Also, bring into play how or if a minority classification either on the part of the diners or the waiter would influence the decision (20). *It may take some courage to add this to the discussion and, of course, respect will be involved.*

2. Using the newspaper advertisements, have students working in groups decide which advertisement gives the customer the best deal. Record decisions and be prepared to explain. Trade with other groups and decide on the best (5, 6, 12,14,16, 27).

3. Homework: Ask the students to report the next day if they thought any television advertisements were less than honest.

Instructional Procedures for Day 3

1. Read several passages from one of Rush Limbaugh's narrations (from the text, *The Bum's Rush*) in which he uses phrases expressing percentages ("There are more Indians alive today than when Columbus discovered America, so how can anyone say we practiced genocide on them?"). Ask the class to relate his statements to mathematical percentages, probable accuracy, *and whether honesty and humility might have a role in the delivery or the interpretation* (6). Have the class choose sides if there is any disagreement, and practice mediation strategies to come to a mutual agreement (28).

2. Homework: Have each student write a letter to the president, newspaper, or company complaining about any advertisement, article, or TV announcement or program that is unfair, dishonest, or prejudicial. This letter should include students' math work (31).

Instructional Procedures for Day 4

1. Bring class, as prearranged, to the local grocery store. Groups stand by each checkout line and offer to help customers carry their bags or push their carts to the parking lot (21). Parents who have volunteered supervise.
2. Each time a group actually helps someone, have it write down (one student should act as recorder) the approximate age, gender, and race of the person who accepted the help.
3. Homework: Have each student write down his or her honest feelings while helping people at the store, and a summary of his or her percent findings relating to gender, age, and race and how many of each group accepted help. Students should include percentages (i.e., percentage of Latinos accepting help) (20).

Closure and Assessment:

On the fifth day, have the groups present what percentage of age, gender, and race accepted help using as many comparisons as possible. Lead class in a discussion about any conclusions that may be drawn.

Have the class relax while listening to soft, classical, or new age music.[5] Have them imagine a world where all people are treated with respect and generosity. Have them imagine always being honest to others and others being honest to them. Tie good feelings to humility.

After bringing students back to the here and now, ask them to assess the week's activities and what they learned. *(Note to reader: Recall that this simple way to end a visualization session ensures that students who drift off return to the present. Otherwise, there is a remote possibility that they may stay in this slightly altered state for a while longer and may be awakened more rudely by someone else later. Also remember that the hypnotic influence of your words occurs whether or not you consciously use visualization strategies, so do not be overly concerned about the many misinterpretations you hear about this phenomenon.)*

Refer back to daily observation notes to assess student outcome in academics and character and record in your grade book and in students' permanent portfolios.

Follow-up Activities and Homework

Ask students to keep a journal over the weekend of how many times they practiced or did not practice humility and honesty during situations that made it difficult to do so. How many times do they encounter percentages?

Personal Reflection

I expected a little controversy from some parents who are Rush Limbaugh fans, and from children of fans, but it did not happen. Of course, the principal had a problem with it, he did not make a big deal about it. Anyway, the students will be more careful about what and whom they believe, and this is worth such critical thinking about an influential talk-show host's words.

The grocery store experience was a multifaceted endeavor that was so full of learning experiences I will use it again.

LESSON PLAN: PLANNING AND HOSTING A PARTY

Title: Planning and Hosting a Party • Academic subject: *Mathematics* • Character subject: *Fortitude, courage, patience, honesty, humility, generosity* • Grade levels: *1–2* • Time allowed: *50 minutes × 4 days* • Date last modified: *5-14-00*	**Learning Goals** Academic: *To practice and apply counting, basic addition, subtraction, multiplication, and division; rhythms and music; organization skills; telling time; comparison; and measurement* Character: *To realize the role of virtues in communication and preparation*	**Official Content Standard Addressed** *Understand numbers, ways of representing numbers, relationships among numbers, and number systems; understand meanings of operations and how they relate to one another; and compute fluently and make reasonable estimates. (NCTM, 2000)*
Specific Objectives Academic: *To count the students in the class, draw diagrams, count guests, count music, organize duties, perform tasks at particular times, quadruple recipes, compare sizes of orange peels, predict the number of peel pieces, recognize fractions of an orange, measure ingredients, and divide food* Character: *To practice courage in the process of personally inviting other staff and students to the party; practice generosity through preparing and sharing food; show fortitude during the party preparations; express courage while providing entertainment; and show humility by accepting construction criticism*		**Resources and Materials** • *simple recipes* • *ingredients and materials for recipes* • *oranges* • *tape deck or CD player for music (students may opt for live music)* • *construction paper* • *cleaning materials*
Student Prerequisite Skills/Knowledge Academic: *Basic knowledge of the whole numbers* Character: *Should know what it means to have courage, fortitude, patience, and humility, and to be generous*	**Opening Questions** Academic: *In what ways do we use math in the real world? We are planning a holiday party. What math skills might we use?* Character: *What virtues are needed to plan a party? What virtues are needed to host a party?*	

Combining these two virtues worked well. No quality stands solely on its own in human behavior and affairs. For example, if assertiveness is to be effective and well received, it should be tempered with respect and kindness. I think we made unconscious connections with this idea in terms of bold advertisements or political statements that are not tempered with honesty or humility.

The real-life applications of percents seemed to help students internalize them.

Maybe next time I could add more math while looking at the amount of money grocery customers spent. I need to be careful not to water down my math content by overemphasizing virtue education.

Sample Lesson 4, Grade Level K–2

Some teachers find it easier to emphasize only one or two virtues in a lesson plan, especially with younger children. Also, many find that generosity and respect may be among the easier virtues to teach to first- and second-graders. However, to illustrate that all the virtues can be taught at any age, we try to use several in this unit.

(Actually, you will see that the teacher who helped us create this lesson plan did plan on using honesty, but because a natural opportunity for it came up, so included it.)

Instructional Procedures for Day 1

1. Decide on a theme for the party. Have the class offer ideas, discuss them, and then reach a consensus on which idea to use (10, 16, 20, 23). *(Note to reader: American Indian forms of government and decision making typically called for consensus rather than majority. This seems to work well for children, as well. It may take more time, but you will find in the long run that it has many benefits. For example, feelings are not be hurt, resentment is minimal, participation is maximized, and, in the process of gaining consensus, many opportunities for teaching and practicing the virtues emerge. Notice how many items from the Checklist come into play, as well.)*

2. Using the same method as above, discuss what type of food will be served, what kind of entertainment will be provided, and who will be invited (5). Remind *the students that hosting a party requires generosity.* Ask them why they think that is true.

3. Have students work in pairs to draw an outline of how the classroom will look during the party (1). Will guests sit at desks? Will people be standing most of the time? Ask students to close their eyes and visualize the party (8). The room probably will have to be rearranged. Ask students to draw the arrangement they would like to see (13).

4. Ask for volunteers to share their diagrams and explain why they chose that particular arrangement. Ask the students if they feel embarrassed to make suggestions about what they think should happen. *If so, relate this to courage.* Note that students may criticize one another's designs. *Have two students role-play to show how to accept criticism with humility (9).*

5. Make a list of things that need to be done. Next, organize the list into categories and form committees (committees can include set-up, supplies, food, entertainment, invitations, and clean-up). Have students sign up for the committee they wish to be a part of.

6. Homework: Those on the food committee should bring in easy recipes from home that

can be made inexpensively and don't need to be cooked (trail mix is a good one). Those on the entertainment committee should bring in ideas for entertainment. They may want to bring sheet music for singing or an audiotape for dancing. A note should be sent home explaining this assignment to parents (19). *Remind students that when a parent or neighbor or friend offers them an item for the party they should express appreciation for this person's generosity.*

Instructional Procedures for Day 2

1. Discuss again who is to be invited. Have students count the number of people in the class and estimate how many will fit comfortably. Ask questions like, "If there are 20 students and we can fit 40 people in the room, how many guests can each child invite?" If this question seems too difficult for students to solve in their head, pass out manipulatives, like beans, and tell the students to imagine that the beans are people. This may help them find a solution. *For first-graders, this will take patience and perseverance, so remind them of these two virtues and what they mean before the children begin.*

2. Children make invitations out of construction paper for guests who are not at the school, and they form small groups to invite in-school site guests personally. *Role-play such an invitation and point out how the virtue of courage can come into play* (9). Suggest that one group create a song about this; perhaps they could even sing it for others (11).

3. Give each committee time to meet and discuss its ideas (23).

4. Each committee should be given time to present its ideas to the class and ask the class for help. *Each group member should present one idea so that all the students have a chance to practice their courage.*

5. Final decisions are made about food and entertainment. For the remainder of this lesson assume that the children decided to dance and sing and serve trail mix and oranges.

6. The food group determines who brings what ingredients. Help the group introduce the following math problem: If the trail mix recipe serves ten people, how much of each ingredient do we need to bring to a party with 40 guests?

> **Trail Mix Recipe**
> 1 cup candy-coated chocolate pieces
> 2 handfuls (5-year-old hands) shredded coconut
> 1 cup sunflower seeds
> 1 cup peanuts
> 5 handfuls raisins

Here, again, manipulatives should be introduced to help students multiply. The teacher should explain the procedure for quadrupling the number of candy pieces and the amount of coconut. Students should be encouraged to figure out how many cups of sunflower seeds and peanuts and how many handfuls of raisins. Teach the class that if anyone notices boredom or frustration, he or she has permission to say the word *perseverance* or *fortitude* out loud, including the child who is feeling frustrated. The class is taught upon hearing that word to sing joyfully, "Don't give up, don't give up, it's going to work out fine!" (11, 25). This should be done with humor and should not be forced on anyone.

7. Ask the students with the song to practice singing the song they selected to perform.
8. Homework: bring in ingredients, bowls, cups, napkins, decorations, etc. Decorations can also be made during art time (22).

Instructional Procedures for Day 3

1. Students practice the dance and song. *Before this, tell a story of a young dancer who struggled with basic steps for years before becoming a professional on Broadway. Ask which virtue this is about* (29).
2. Make the trail mix.
3. The teacher gives a short lesson on the math of an orange. Here students can predict the number of peel pieces that will result, they can compare the sizes of the pieces, and they can see the fractional parts of the orange (the slices). This should be presented in a lecture/discussion format. *Ask the children what virtue(s) comes into play when peeling an orange.* Peel all of the oranges and store for the next day.

Instructional Procedures for Day 4

1. Decorate and set up the room.
2. Divide the trail mix into small cups for each guest.
3. Ask the students how many different ways they can show generosity to their guests. Ask, "How can we show courage?" One response might be, "to thank them for coming." Another might be *"it takes courage to show them our dance routine."* Each student should have a chance to greet guests at the door to practice his or her courage and generosity.
4. Perform song and dance.
5. Encourage students to explain/demonstrate for their guests the math that was used to plan and host this party. *What virtues do they get to practice?*
6. Remind students to thank their guests for coming as they leave.
7. Finally, discuss clean-up. Find out who doesn't like to clean his or her room. Why is this? (Because it takes forever, it's hard, I have to ask for help, sometimes I have my dirty clothes in the closet, etc.) *At each response, see if the children can determine which virtue comes into play (patience, perseverance, humility, honesty).*

Closure and Assessment

Since all of the guests were adult staff members, I was able to use them as assessment tools. When the guests arrived, I handed them a card. Listed on one side were all the instances that a student may have used one of the six virtues. On the other side was a list of the math skills. When the students are asked to share their learning experience with their guest (#5 on day 4), the guest has the "cheat sheet." He or she can give immediate feedback to the child and the teacher. The teacher should walk around and monitor this process.

Personal Reflection

There were so many people that the students wanted to invite, perhaps we can do it again at the end of the year and invite others.

We need to leave more time for clean-up next time.

The kids really liked making decorations; next time we will spend more time doing this and maybe bring math and history into the artwork.

I like when an unforeseen opportunity to teach character education presents itself. I had not planned on discussing honesty during this lesson, but when Sara confessed that sometimes she hides her messy room in the closet or under the bed, I was able to.

The kids got a little silly when we sang the "perseverance song." I am glad they enjoyed it; however, some were taking advantage of it and shouting, "perseverance," when it was not necessary. Next time, I will discuss the virtue of honesty before this activity. The students can only shout, "perseverance," when it is appropriate.

Notes

1. Don Jacobs lived with the Raramuri people and learned from his experiences in their land about the CAT-FAWN Connection. These experiences are described in his book, *Primal Awareness* (1998).

2. This refers to the seven directions: the sacred aspects of the four cardinal directions, the sky above, the earth below, and the center of self. The number four is a sacred number for most American Indian tribes or nations. An Oglala Lakota man named Tyon explains why:

In former times the Lakota grouped all their activities by fours. This was because they recognized four directions: the west, the north, the east and the south; four division of time: the day, the night, the moon, and the year; four parts in everything that grows from the ground: the roots, the stem, the leaves, and the fruit; four kinds of things that breathe: those that crawl, those that fly, those that walk on four legs, and those that walk on two legs; four things above the world: the great spirit, the associates of the great spirit, the spirits below them and the spirit-kin; four periods of human life: babyhood, childhood, adulthood, and old age; and finally, mankind has four fingers on each hand, four toes on each foot and the thumbs and the great toes taken together form four. Since the Great Spirit caused everything to be in fours, mankind should do everything possible in fours. (Radin, P. (1927). *Primitive Man as Philosopher* (New York: D. Appleton, p. 278).

3. Find reference for this (National Council of Teachers).

4. About Teaching Mathematics. (2000). Math Solutions Publications. Sausalito, CA, p. 29.

5. Recall that research indicates that certain kinds of background music, like classical music played by stringed instruments at 60 beats per minute, can enhance concentration. We keep a CD player handy and use it often. Children may not like it at first, since classical is not generally their kind of music, but they usually come to like it. They even often ask us to play it when we forget.

Chapter 10

The Visual and Performing Arts

*Indigenous arts provided and continue to provide a foundational way
to express and nourish the soul of the instinctual human need to learn and create.*
— Gregory Cajete, *Look to the Mountain*

*When people have a ceremony done for them, it relaxes their body;
it relaxes their mind; it—you might say—takes them into
another world for a while and, if they give their full attention, they can be healed.*
— Traditional indigenous wisdom

Alternative Visions of Reality

Everything that is perceived by the senses is an aspect of reality in the American Indian worldview. Art in all of its forms reflects this sensual dimension of existence. For both the artist and the audience, song, dance, paintings, drama, and other creative expressions play an important role in symbolizing the congruence of a multifaceted universe. In feeling the interconnections, one may be transformed in body, mind, and spirit.

The transformational potential of drama, art, and music courses is enhanced when we attach awareness of the core universal virtues. In indigenous thinking, it may be an absurdity to think that there ever could have been a detachment in the first place. But this is because native people have always seen art as a necessary part of life, not as an extracurricular activity reserved for the specially talented. Art always evokes feelings or images that, at some level of consciousness, relate to courage, fortitude, humility, truthfulness, patience, generosity, and other virtues.

For schools to ignore the arts or replace them with more economically or technology oriented courses violates our souls' need for expression. It prevents our students from engaging fully in the processes needed to recreate society in ways that support dynamic and harmonious interrelationships. Villaverde[1] says, "The unconscious and conscious internalizations and expressions of art force reflections and intuitive reactions that are hard to ignore. Art allows for a personal involvement in school, helping to alleviate the alienation and meaninglessness many students feel. When art, critical pedagogy, power, and youth intersect, possibilities expand, differences can be pursued, and a pedagogy of hope and imagination can emerge."

The format for teaching virtues across the curriculum we have presented in earlier chapters for regular academic subjects works equally well when teaching any of the arts. Virtues can be brought into the picture as they relate to historical perspectives of the artwork or artist, sacred aspects of the art, or interpretations and expressions of the art. They also naturally associate with student requirements for learning or participating in the various arts. The more obvious of these includes the courage to perform before an audience; the patience and fortitude to master an instrument; the opportunity for truthful expression; the genuine sharing of self with others as a vehicle for generosity; and the humility that comes when performer or audience truly becomes one with the expression.

Sociodrama

In the dramatic arts is a popular approach to theater that, in effect, uses our approach to character education across the curriculum. It is sometimes referred to as *sociodrama* and was developed by Brazilian theatre director Augusto Boal during the 1950s and 1960s. In an effort to transform theater from the monologue of traditional performance into a dialogue between audience and stage, Boal experimented with many kinds of interactive theater. His explorations were based on the assumption that dialogue is the common, healthy dynamic between all humans. In the same way the authoritarian, "feed the empty bank" forms of teaching are disempowering, Boal asserts that when a dialogue becomes a monologue it ultimately oppresses the people in the audience.

Students who participate in what Boal calls Theater of the Oppressed learn to evaluate, question, and change the scripted play constantly. People in the audience who are watching a skit can interrupt and exchange places with an actor or actress to try the scene another way or give it a different slant or outcome. Students are challenged to truly listen and feel. Numerous exercises are designed to heighten the senses and demechanize the body, to get us out of habitual behavior as a prelude to moving beyond our habitual thinking and interacting. Students interact with other participants, developing relationships and trust and having fun at the same time.

When using this or any other way to teach acting, whether focusing on technique or specific roles, bringing universal virtues onto the scene whenever teachable moments for a particular virtue emerge is a powerful way to help students make the comprehensive experiential connections that ultimately lead to good character.

Music

Indigenous stories of origin from around the world contend that the Great Spirit used music to create the universe. American Indians generally do not see music as a form of entertainment. Songs are entities that define place, offer gratitude, remind people of great things, ask for help, or otherwise serve as a communion with God. They also tend to refocus attention from individualistic concerns to group identity. Musical interaction enables experiences of mutual support and empathy that are not possible with ordinary, rational language.[2]

In western culture people also have recognized the power of music, but more as it relates to inspiration. Many men have marched off to war, inspired by the drum and fife, bagpipes, or Marine Corps hymn. On a more constructive note, songs have inspired people to stop pollution of rivers and turn people away from war. In any event, the emotional, social, and cultural manifestations of music make it fertile ground for teaching virtues. Using the forms from chapter 2 and the format we have been using throughout the book, create a two- to three-session unit that uses the following criteria and information.

Lesson Plan Exercise

The purpose of this unit is for students to learn about one another, learn how to write lyrics, and create songs that could be used as organizing tools for some cause. Goals and objectives relate to learning how folk songs are used with organizing efforts; to gain practice in singing and leading songs; to creating songs collectively about a group and its struggles; and to carry a familiar melody with different words. Materials you will need include paper and pencils, several rhyming dictionaries, and, if possible, a musical instrument or more to accompany singing. *(Note to reader or student teacher: Come up with a title, academic and character goals and objectives, opening questions, and a state standard from your state that relates to the goals and write them in your lesson plan. Be sure to choose a grade level and prerequisites so the language of your procedures is age appropriate. If you know which virtues you plan to incorporate into the lessons, fill in the character goals and objectives now. Or wait until after you see which ones emerge while you write the instructional procedures.)*

Instructional Procedures

1. Ask the students to think about a song they know and like. Then have them take turns introducing themselves, telling what their song is, and explaining why they like it. Allow about one minute for this. If the student is comfortable, ask him or her to sing the chorus or a verse of the song. *(Note to reader: Elaborate a little on this instruction in your own words using the Pedagogy and Procedures Checklist to help you think of different things to do. Write the number of the strategy from the Checklist used in this first procedure. While you are doing this, remember that your intention is to create opportunities for bring an awareness of one of the virtues into play, or directly or indirectly planting seeds for spiritual awareness. Insert sentences that will remind you of what to say or how to make the connection with the students and underline it, making sure that the specific virtue is mentioned also. Do this for each of the procedures below, as well.)*

2. Have the students think of some folk songs that have come from or contributed to organizing efforts. Be prepared to guide them in remembering those songs. Use a variety of research and media tools if necessary to come up with some representative songs. Examples are "We Shall Overcome," and "Which Side Are You On?"

3. Discuss folk songs you and the group identify in terms of the specific struggles, hopes, or dreams of people; the uniting qualities of the song; how the song was not controlled by elite interests but by the common people; etc. Ask the students if any current issues relate to the goals of the song. *(Note to reader: What virtues were displayed by the people who wrote these songs, and what virtues were not demonstrated in the environment in which they were written?)*

4. Ask the students what types of things they would like to write an organizing song about and why. *(Note to reader: Is student ownership addressed here? If so, jot the number down from the Checklist. When students own the subject, the virtues are more likely to play a role when they talk about "why.")* Such things as closing a toxic dump, improving schools, joining a group to save the whales, etc., are ideas.

5. Then have the students choose a song with a familiar melody they can use with the new lyrics. These can come from commercial jingles, popular folk songs, Christmas carols, etc. (They can use an original melody if the group has the background and skills to do so.) *(Note to reader: Can you use critical thinking here? Perhaps a commercial jingle deserves some brief analysis if it is a bit far-fetched, for example. If you can use critical thinking somehow, what virtues would arise from so doing?)* Divide the students into groups of three and have some groups come up with a chorus and others come up with some verses for the song. Guide students toward a song message that has a main point for the chorus.

The words in the song should be meaningful and understandable to all. Suggest humor, rhyming words, etc.

6. Explain that verses should have two lines with the last words of each line rhyming, and that the chorus should have four lines with the last words of the second and fourth lines rhyming.

7. When the first drafts are done, have each group look over the song together and modify it to make it more singable or its message clearer. After the final draft is completed, type it out on the computer and distribute copies to everyone, with the versus numbered in the order they will be sung.

8. Ask for volunteers to lead the group in singing the song and encourage everyone to participate in singing. Each group can sing the verse it wrote, and the entire group can sing the chorus. Try adding clapping, musical instruments, and harmony. After singing it several times, see if the class wants to make any changes. If changes are recommended, permission must be given from the group that wrote the original words.

9. Practice and give a performance before an appropriate audience.

We hope you were able to use a variety of pedagogical strategies and at least four or five good opportunities to talk about or make students aware of related virtues. If so, you are ready to turn your own lesson plans into moral development exercises or you can now create lesson plans with both the academic subject and the virtue in mind.

Notes

1. Villaverde, 2000, p. 188.
2. See *Primal Awareness*, p. 217, for more on indigenous aspects of music.

Part 4
The Mysteries of the West

Chapter 11

Not to Be Remiss

Richard M. Jones

> *The history of the white society in regard*
> *to Indian education reflects the drama of the inexorable peopling*
> *of this continent by those unable or unwilling to establish and*
> *maintain a humane, fraternal, and consistently respectful*
> *relationship with the prior residents of the land.*
> — Estelle Fuchs and Robert Havighurst,
> *To Live on This Earth*

The goal of this book has been to encourage teachers, teachers of teachers, teacher candidates, and anyone else interested in the welfare of children to approach character education by weaving virtue awareness and development into daily discourse. With this purpose in mind one can continually recognize teachable moments for imbuing virtues awareness into the curriculum. A citizenship grade on a report card does not constitute character education. Good character development requires that parents and teachers cooperate to provide lessons in character that are meaningful by ensuring they are in the proper context, and that they are associated with relevant examples and actual deeds. This requirement is a challenge in itself, yet there are even more subtle challenges.

In chapter 1, the authors provide powerful resources to assist you. Yet this book would be remiss if it did not discuss some of the more intriguing and specific challenges a teacher faces when integrating the study of values into the standard curriculum. The first relates to the pedagogical practice of behaviorism that tends to stifle an experiential, integrated approach to character education. Because character education must be taught with sincere intention, the absence of predisposition is detrimental to an effective program. Behaviorists emphasize reinforcement strategies that produce the behaviors predetermined by the educator or curriculum. Behaviorism lacks the predisposition to encourage the open-ended discussion and critical thinking that character education requires. Behaviorism is mechanistic, and a philosophy of machines is no way to treat a child.

Standardized Testing Revisited

Behaviorist pedagogy is measured appropriately by standardized testing. School reform efforts have emphasized serious paradigm shifts in our pedagogical practices, yet standardized testing remains *the tool* for measuring student progress. This incompatibility ultimately stifles reform potential. In this regard, like most things in life, we, as teachers and administrators, are our own worst enemies. If we do not understand the consequences of a standardized test mentality, we will also be the greatest challenge to effective character education.

Our sample lesson plans have demonstrated that character education does not need an expensive program and that it works best if one does not take a prescriptive "Value of the

Month Club" approach. Virtue awareness must be a part of one's everyday considerations to have a lasting effect. The traditional emphasis on retention of facts presents a great challenge to this goal. Because teachers are caught up in teaching content and are under extreme pressure to get through the textbook, a behaviorist approach to teaching that substitutes classroom management for character development is understandable, albeit unfortunate.

Confusing good education, and especially good character education, with good and measurable behavior is a common problem in schools currently advocating such education. One need not use a particular pedagogical approach to be successful in teaching virtues. However, virtues flourish in an environment that recognizes the need for children to construct knowledge based on their accumulated and critically considered experience. The behaviorist tool of standardized testing does not measure such an environment adequately. Standardized testing is best used to measure what has been described as the "banking concept of education." According to Paulo Freire,[1] "It is not surprising that the banking concept of education regards people as adaptable, manageable beings. However, the more students work at storing the deposits entrusted to them, the less they develop the critical consciousness which would result from their intervention in the world as transformers of that world."

A constructivist approach encourages students to construct meaning from experience and the students' own interpretation of that experience. However, constructivism is not sufficient to overcome current barriers to teaching virtues. We must also be aware that cultural and ecological precepts give meaning to experience. A strictly constructivist view, if it ignores western culture's ideal of individuality, can lead to a sort of relativism and to an anthropocentric view of the world.[2] With such a view, true spiritual awareness is difficult to gain. If we base our character strictly on meanings we have constructed on our road to autonomy, then virtues like generosity may become more about personal benefit than genuine caring.

Combining the constructivist view with an ecological and cultural awareness characterizes the essence of Native American approaches to learning. It illustrates the dance between individuality and community and ecosystems. Constructivism is naturally predisposed to cooperative education, thematic units, learning centers, and the startling concept of the teacher as co-learner and facilitator. Through real-life problem posing and discussion, education becomes a liberating experience rather than a subjugating one. Autonomy is valued, but not at the expense of community or environment. Students learn what it means to be human and how people can transform themselves into better beings through reflection on experience.

The specter of standardized testing diminishes character education because it minimizes the importance of reflecting on knowledge, questioning knowledge, expanding knowledge, and thinking critically about how knowledge relates to virtue and good character. It has served to confuse our national education policy. On one hand, school reform is calling for a multifaceted approach to measuring student performance. On the other, state and national legislators are insisting on accountability for student learning and see standardized tests as the quick and easy way to measure student knowledge. The two conflict with one another. Standardized testing measures one thing: an individual's performance of knowledge at a particular moment of time. It measures the acquisition of facts.

As was pointed out in the chapter on assessments, authentic learning calls for a host of assessment measures. The emphasis is on the individual child, not on the child compared with other children. Assessments are directed at improving the individual child's skills and abilities. The focus is on the use of knowledge, not the acquisition of knowledge. It is much like shifting the focus from teaching curriculum to teaching children. When a teacher focuses on children, assessments are formative. When a teacher focuses on curriculum, the assessments become summative.

Ultimately, our almost exclusive focus on summative assessments has turned us away from an optimal approach to teaching. It has fragmented character education and separated it from academic education. It has even served to promote such unethical practices as cheating at all levels to avoid the high-stake risks now attached to test scores.

Colleagues

Another specific challenge we would be remiss in ignoring, one perhaps more indirect and enigmatic than succumbing to the standardized tests movement, can be found among our fellow colleagues. In times of uncertainty people often cling tenaciously to uncertain ideologies. Change is a fearsome affair and engenders a kind of suspicion that impedes progress. School reform has brought into question the many long-held ideologies that support the "banking" system of education. But this form of teaching is comfortable to too many teachers and administrators. Anyone who tries to disturb this comfort zone is likely to be separated and ostracized or criticized.

Too many of our teachers are the products of a "paternalistic system . . . colonized by a dominant, hierarchical district."[3] Such teachers are often "codependent" and "compliant." This type of teacher is highly resistant to change and adheres to the status quo. In most cases, introducing character education into the curriculum will be upsetting to the codependent teacher. What is alarming about this dysfunction is that it is usually the veteran teacher who is most steadfast and "uses their influence to maintain the status quo, even to the point of acculturating new teachers into those norms."[4]

New teachers, fresh from college and prepared to use character education, learning centers, thematic units, cooperative learning, multi-age level teaching, critical inquiry, and a variety of assessment procedures often find themselves in foreign territory. Eventually, the system manipulates and finally acculturates them into the so-called real way of doing things. It takes a teacher of exceptional character to withstand isolation amidst a dysfunctional community of teachers, but that is just the teacher who can integrate character education into the classroom successfully.

Administration

Although administrators are also colleagues, they can represent a separate category of challenges to consider. Poor administrators do not take special classes designed to increase ability to suppress innovation or good teaching. They have fallen victim to an authoritarian system, as have the rest of us involved in education. School reform rhetoric has recognized the problems with the authoritarian structure of our educational system and addresses it with several possible avenues of redress. Site-based management moves the individual school out from under the direct hierarchical control of the district and hints at the principal sharing power. The leadership team concept brings the idea of teachers proactively participating in the governance of their school a little closer to realization. Unfortunately, few administrators are able to walk this talk. Recognizing the codependency discussed earlier between administrators and teachers reveals the complexity of giving up or sharing power. Few systems build within themselves the structures that prove to be their demise. Power tends to seek aggregation; it seldom disseminates itself.

School Boards with Private Agendas

A school or district can be only as good as its administrators, but administrators can only be as good as the school board lets them be. Mark Twain once said that there was nothing more irritating than a good example. If terms like "honesty, openness, ethics, and standards" describe the school board that operates in your district, school reform and character education will not be so difficult. But, all too frequently, if the education leaders of a district do not practice the values associated with good character themselves, character education is not likely to blossom in the classroom. The inconsistencies would be too obvious. "Honesty, openness and fairness are words that are often used by school board members, but the 'good-old-boy' practice continues throughout the country. This is a practice where honesty, openness, ethics, equity, fairness and standards are ignored for the purpose of helping one's compatriots so that they in turn can provide help."[5]

The good-old-boy network openly conflicts with the precepts of cultivating virtues. This obvious dissonance places character education at risk or, at least, in a highly ambiguous position. The good old boys tolerate substandard behavior(s) from their members. A good old boy can borrow school property permanently, miss important meetings, ignore policy, gossip about teachers, and undermine the school culture with little fear of consequences. School board influences prevent discipline or restrict discipline from being applied to its fullest extent. The school board ends up supporting the kinds of employees, often referred to as toxic employees, who poison the school atmosphere. This is an atmosphere that makes character education a clandestine activity.

This conflict with administrators and school board members is the most difficult and dealing with them requires the most courage and the most honesty. School administrators and school board members play political games with teachers, community members, and, most reprehensible, with children to accomplish their end goals. While the school board may support school reform, technology enhancement, a globalized curriculum, constructivism, and character education publicly, in the background and behind closed doors the elements necessary to implement these various programs may be subverted. The funds may not be allocated. The staff training will be remiss. The community will be opposed. The administration will fail in its leadership role to actively encourage the programs. Using these covert methods to undermine a program then allows the administration and/or the school board to say, "We tried it, but it just didn't seem to work."

In a school where the school board has overstepped its authority and works towards its own agenda(s) and not for the children's welfare, the climate is one of fear, resentment, and indecision. Board members engaged in pursuing private agendas tend to micromanage school affairs. Micromanagement debilitates administrators, infuriates teachers, and incarcerates students, holding them hostage to political favors, personality clashes, and the inappropriate professionalism of making education decisions based on political expediency rather than on real research in education.

Students are being held accountable by antiquated, industrial-age standardized testing to prove that schools are teaching what needs to be taught. One might ask rhetorically who is deciding what children should be taught. Too often it is not the professional educators who have devoted their lives to researching real and practical curriculums and pedagogical practices. This is why the great ideas discussed at national workshops seldom are initiated at the classroom level. No incentive exists. In fact, the opposite is true. Penalties often exist for attempting to engage students in an education that actively involves them.

There are ways to counteract this type of poolroom politics. The first is not to react to it by participating in it. Avoid finger pointing and gossip. Set out to change the system without attacking anyone. Gather your courage, stay honest, and be a role model for others. If you truly believe in authentic character education, then implement it openly. Invite parents into initial discussions about selecting universal virtues. Ask them to come to the classroom to see how you teach these values. Involve the community in interactive learning opportunities with your class. Implement service-learning projects and encourage your students to engage in civic activities. Be an inclusive classroom in the best sense of the word.

Hidden Curriculum

What is taught in school is often more subtle than reading, writing, and arithmetic. In a very real sense dominant culture is encoded in everything that happens in the classroom, and this invisible influence often contradicts the intentions of pedagogy or curriculum. For example, you may try to use cooperative learning, but the culture's emphasis on competition over cooperation and individuality over the group will speak louder than your efforts. A teacher can reinforce dominant culture values within the classroom inadvertently and not be aware of it.

Institutional racism is one example of the subtleties of dominant culture and the hidden curriculum. This racism finds expression in gender bias and the obvious color bias. The hidden curriculum "is the unexpressed perpetuation of the dominant culture through institutional processes."[6] The hidden curriculum often deprives minority children, females, and other marginalized human beings of culture, language and differing perspectives on events both past and present.

This underlying reinforcement of dominant culture has a direct affect on the practice of virtues and underlines the importance of student and community involvement in establishing what virtues are examined and how these values are defined. Important questions in history and current controversies are shaded with uninvestigated values. Sometimes, while discussing controversial issues, viewpoints arise that are counter to commonly held assumptions. This presents an opportunity to discuss many deep and thought-provoking questions, but there may be repercussions for uncovering that which may have been obscured purposefully. A possible way to resolve this hidden curriculum problem is with a different worldview that may help redirect the negative assumptions of our culture; this book has suggested the American Indian perspective as a viable alternative.

The Students

The students themselves may not respond well to character education initially. Talking about respect, caring, honesty, courage, and responsibility is personal. Most students have learned to hide feelings that may leave them vulnerable to others, or worse, they have learned to ignore their inner voice and disregard prompts that denote caring, honesty, and other character traits. It is touchy ground when one begins to expose inner feelings. It is very difficult to discuss ideals held close to one's heart publicly. Often, one who is seen as wearing his heart on his sleeve is perceived as being weak or a sissy.

Discussing issues of character honestly can be seen as approaching personal boundaries, which may set in motion a series of fronts, feints, and other distractions to avoid possible encroachment. Students, especially adolescents, are experts at erecting defense mechanisms to redirect perceived threats to their inner selves. Character issues unintentionally may trigger strong defensive reactions from students. Anger, derision, ridicule, and cynicism may be the first response to character education across the curriculum.

Some of our children may come from backgrounds that openly conflict with the defined virtues you are hoping to encourage. For a student to embrace humility or courage when these have lost their value in the home environment is not an easy task. Generosity may be seen as a weakness in families that struggle for existence and promote selfish viewpoints. The problems of drugs, gangs, and early promiscuity have hardly been overstated. What appear to us as problems are often seen as solutions by young people. Values have become twisted and closed. Honesty may be practiced, but only within the closed peer group. Respect is reserved for power. Students tend to align themselves with those perceived as being strong. Their concept of sharing and caring is then limited. This distortion results in a limited or even false application of values.

By Way of a Summary

School reform has at its heart the development of the whole child first, development of the staff second, and improvement of the institution third. It is character that builds the child, enhances the staff, and enriches the institution. Educators cannot let legislators determine educational goals and outcomes, and they should not let testing companies determine assessment protocols. Nor can they allow school boards to give nothing more than lip service to school reform. As efforts at school reform fail across the country, and accountability for the failure begins to surface, school boards may begin to find more than the occasional finger pointing in their direction.

Schools are among the most autocratic institutions in America. Too often they are governed by an oligarchy of ill-intentioned political aspirants who actively pursue private agendas. Administrators will find themselves responding to teachers and students in the same manner in which they are treated. If they are commanded, they command. If they are micromanaged, they micromanage. If they allow themselves to be treated as though their expertise is meaningless, they treat others as though the others are meaningless.

Teachers suffer the consequences of this complex cycle of oppression. It is degenerative and builds dysfunctional relationships. Teachers move away from controversy, avoid confrontation, and complain incessantly to those who will listen. They teach mechanically and joylessly. The classroom is a place to learn facts and skills. It is not a place where children are encouraged to express themselves or find out about things that are not in the textbook and the accompanying workbook pages.

Students learning about democracy in a school in America are like Indian children learning about being parents at a boarding school. It is talked about but seldom demonstrated in a valid way. The hidden curriculum tells the true story. The intentionality of democracy is missing, just as understanding family life is missing in a boarding school. It may well be that the true goal is to deform the process of democracy just as the intention of the boarding school was to change the traditional family life of the Native American radically. Schools may be oppressive and authoritarian for a purpose. The threat that whole-school reform presents may hinder its chances of success. School boards would have to stop manipulating the system to meet their own selfish and personal agendas. Administrators would have to give up power and build leadership within the schools among teachers and noncertified personnel. Teachers would have to take power and spend time developing their leadership capacity. They would have to learn how to cooperate and team with one another. Teachers would become reflective practitioners of critical pedagogy and would commit to character education. With teachers initiating these changes, students might break the habit of boredom that defines too many current school routines.

All of these things happen when character becomes at least as important as curriculum, and adults practice the universal values of courage, honesty, respect, humility, humor, generosity, and caring. Courage is vital when broaching subjects close to one's heart, where our values should be. A little honesty in the curriculum would open doors to understanding our nation and our selves. Respect for children as anxious learners and explorers, and respect for oneself and one's profession, too often missing. Humility makes us able to learn from our students, to relearn for ourselves, and to unlearn some presumptions that need to be discarded. Humor allows us to laugh with our students and at ourselves. Generosity and caring are why we are in this profession. We all hope to use the gift of communication to learn and grow with our children in a caring and ethical atmosphere

Our natural instincts, as revealed in the educational processes of indigenous people around the globe, are to be caring, patient, and kind with our children. The barriers to good character development in our children ultimately are a result of having allowed these instincts to be replaced or misdirected. We know this and we talk about it constantly. It's time to stop talking and start walking.

Notes

1. Freire, 1999, p. 54.
2. Bowers, 2000, pp. 46–49.
3. Lambert, 1998, p. 35.
4. Ibid., p. 34.
5. Flinchbaugh, 1993, p. 130.
6. Wink, 2000, p. 54.

Chapter 12

The Ten Commandments?

You may think now that you own God as you wish to
own our land, but you cannot. Our God is the same God.
— Chief Seattle, in his 1854 speech

On February of the year 2000, Pope John Paul II said that
"The Ten Commandments provide the only true basis
for the lives of individuals, societies and nations.
Is this not the same belief that contributed the genocide of my people?
— A Lakota elder, spoken at a community meeting

In 1999, The U.S. House of Representatives voted 248 to 180 to allow states to post the Ten Commandments in public schools. This rider was attached to a juvenile justice crime bill. Its author convinced the legislators that only an improvement in the morality of youth can prevent the violent crimes they are perpetrating, and that biblical laws are the best source for such a task. Since federal and state legislation has pointed toward the Ten Commandments as an allowable or a required approach to character education, brief discussion on the valid role of this policy in character education is important to the goals of this book.[1]

To date, 14 states have passed laws either allowing or mandating that schools post the ten biblical mandates in all classrooms. For example, the Colorado government passed Senate Bill 114, which states: "Each school district shall post in every public school classroom and in the main entryway in every public school a durable and permanent copy of the Ten Commandments as specified in paragraph (b) of this subsection." Similarly, Georgia's House Bill 1207 amends Georgia's Quality Basic Education Act to require local school systems to ensure that the Ten Commandments are displayed in every classroom within the school district, "as a condition for receiving state funds" (House Bill 1207).

As character educators, we must consider carefully the possible repercussions of this growing public policy that endorses the Ten Commandments as the only true basis for our children's lives. Where they are mandated, we should take advantage of the situation and use it in the most optimal way for teaching virtues. It is best if we begin with such questions as, "Will the practice of posting (and presumably explaining) the Ten Commandments enhance or confuse moral development?" "Now that we have been asked to post the Ten Commandments in our classroom, how can we best study them to help our students grow into people with good character?"

The following are some sample questions you can use (modifying for age relevancy) to stimulate critical thinking about core universal virtues. The first question after the commandment challenges the appropriateness and priorities of the particular commandment. The second tries to use the commandment's intent in a constructive, character-building way. (Although we believe that the Ten Commandments are more about religious orthodoxy than a way to truly develop core universal virtues, we ask the second question to give great benefit of the doubt to the interpretations.)

(Note: There are three versions of the Ten Commandments in the Hebrew Scriptures [Old Testament]: Exodus 20:2–18, Exodus 334:12–26, and Deuteronomy 5:6–21. Exodus is the most commonly used [King James Version].)

The First Commandment: *Thou shalt have no other gods before me.*

Does the first commandment, which demands that only the Hebrew God be worshipped, convey respect for diversity and multicultural perspectives?

Could we interpret this to mean that we should believe in one divine creator and not worship such false gods as money or fame?

The Second Commandment: *Thou shalt not make unto thee any graven image, or any likeness of any thing that is in heaven above, or that is in the earth beneath, or that is in the water under the earth. Thou shalt not serve them for I am a jealous God, visiting the iniquity of the fathers upon the children unto the third and fourth generation. . . .*

Might a mandate against any object of worship create confusion or unnecessary guilt in children who themselves or whose parents create or otherwise use sacred symbols (like the American Indian pipe)? And what can we say about jealousy and threats of punishment in light of moral development, including punishment of future generations?

Could this mean that worship should only be for the great mysterious Spirit, and we should never be so arrogant as to think we can reduce this Spirit into an image? Could the authors have read in their own human emotions about jealousy and punishment?

The Third Commandment: *Thou shalt not take the name of the Lord they God in vain, for the Lord will not hold him guiltless that taketh his name in vain.*

The original interpretation of this related to breaking contracts that were sworn on God's name. More recently people have come to think this means not cursing with God's name ("gosh darn" probably does not count). In either case, might this ultimate law somehow detract from an emphasis on the great universal virtues that emphasize generosity, humility, courage, etc.?

Could this just be telling us to be very truthful always, but especially if we invoke God's name?

The Fourth Commandment: *Remember the Sabbath day, to keep it holy. Six days shalt thou labour and do all thy work, But the seventh day is the Sabbath of the Lord thy God: in it thou shalt not do any work. . . .*

Since the Sabbath originally referred to Saturday, is a mandate not to work on Saturday going to contribute seriously to the moral development of young people?

Do you think that in our modern world we could use this as a reminder to slow down and spend more time in spiritual pursuits and less in material ones?

The Fifth Commandment: *Honor thy father and thy mother that thy days may be long upon the land. . . .*

From a critical thinking standpoint, is it a violation of the mandate to honor one's father and mother if a child's father has abused, molested, and violated the child and continues to do so? If a young person has such good reason not to honor a parent, is it healthy to expect that this person's life may be cut short by God? If we generally respect all people, is it wise to be more selective in which ones we honor?

Is it not a good idea to remember all the good things our parents do and show respect for their good work and love?

The Sixth Commandment: *Thou shalt not kill.*

What is the difference between *killing* as in hunting, and *murder*? Is it inconsistent if the same state that mandates the teaching or posting of this law also mandates capital punishment?

If this originally referred to murder, what do you think it would say about capital punishment?

The Seventh Commandment: *Thou shalt not steal.*

Can anyone name a situation where stealing to survive may not be one of the top ten violations of good character? (For older students, some research on this commandment will reveal it originally referred to kidnapping people into slavery, and perhaps this could be discussed.)

Do you think this commandment reflects a practical violation of some of our core universal virtues? Which of our core universal virtues would be violated if someone stole from another?

The Eighth Commandment: *Thou shalt not commit adultery.*

Without condoning adultery, and while being very clear about the reasons it is wrong in our culture, ask about the character of the 40 percent of U.S. adults who have caused this infraction and see if there are any times when adultery might be committed by someone with good character or when it might not rank as one of the top ten morality issues in the world.

With diseases like AIDS, does this mandate now have life and death repercussions if not followed?

The Ninth Commandment: *Thou shalt not bear false witness against thy neighbor.*

Is this reference to honesty complete enough? For example, is it just as bad to be dishonest to oneself or about events as it is to "bear false witness" against neighbors? In other words, are the other ways to be dishonest as well that might be included in this law?

Could this be telling us that the worse form of dishonesty occurs when we hurt another?

The Tenth Commandment: *Thou shalt not covet.*

Are we breaking a serious code of moral conduct and good character if we wish for or desire (covet) someone else's possessions but take no actions in support of such feelings?

Since how and what we think are too often reflected in how we act, could this commandment not motivate us to try and control our desires as much as our actions?

By using both types of questions, one criticizing the efficacy of the Ten Commandments, and one supporting them, a healthy dialogue among teachers, parents, administrators, and students can occur, regardless of religious persuasion. Whatever personal conclusions people make, a better understanding of the virtues could result. In the final analysis, however, we maintain that a school policy that mandates posting the Ten Commandments is more of a boondoggle than a boon for effective character education. We do not mean to be disrespectful of any religion, of course. In fact, like all religious codes, the Commandments have something to offer all of us. For example, "The Jewish laws represent a very clear and passionate understanding of how everything depends on God."[2] Nonetheless, we do not believe that they are the only basis for living or that legislative mandates to publish them in school help promote good character and decrease violence.

If it is helpful to have a code of moral laws posted and explained in classrooms, and it probably is, in keeping with our American Indian worldview, we suggest something like Joe Vlesti's poster of "The Ten Indian Commandments." We invite the reader to formulate similar questions about them to challenge or verify their efficacy and role in promoting good character. Contrast and compare the two sets of rules to live by, not as a way to see which religion or culture is better, but which set better identifies and articulates the universal virtues and which is least likely to discriminate against religious diversity.

The Ten Indian Commandments
1. Treat the Earth and all that dwell thereon with respect.
2. Remain close to the Great Spirit.
3. Show great respect for your fellow beings.
4. Work together for the benefit of all mankind.
5. Give assistance and kindness wherever needed.
6. Do what you know in your heart and mind to be right.
7. Look after the well-being of mind and body.
8. Dedicate a share of your efforts to the greater good.
9. Be truthful and honest at all times.
10. Take responsibility for your actions.

(Joe Vlesti Associates 1993)

Notes

1. This may be even more important consideration of the fact that most of the most prominent forces in character education come from a Catholic persuasion. Although they may or may not agree with the role of Ten Commandments in character education, this increases a need for open discussion and critical thinking.

2. Personal letter to the authors from Jamie Moran. Jamie, a lecturer in psychology, is of Cherokee and Irish blood who believes passionately that most people interpret morality from authoritarian, liberal, or superior orientations that ignore the deep heart's struggle with existence.

Chapter 13

Learning Virtues in Higher Education

Colleges are confused about their mission and how to impart
shared values on which the vitality of both higher education and society depend.
— Ernest Boyer, *College: The Undergraduate Experience in America*

Institutions are projections of what goes on in the human heart.
— Parker Palmer, *To Know As We Are Known*

Is it better to do what is right or to do what will sell?
— Lakota elder, spoken at a community meeting

The University of the Future

One important way to ensure that K–12 schools emphasize character education across the curriculum is to transform institutions of higher education with this priority in mind. To illustrate the importance of this, consider the ultimate influence of college on lower schools. For example, assume we agree that giving letter grades in school is not as effective as using narrative assessments, and that competitive grading, like standardized testing, does more to impede genuine learning than to encourage it. It would be difficult for K–12 schools to implement a no-grading policy unless colleges generally did this also. Currently, colleges use grade point averages as an admittance criterion, so most high schools are forced to use grades. Because high schools use grades, elementary schools also are compelled to do so in their effort to prepare students for future success. In other words, the whole system could be transformed eventually if it began with college. If all colleges taught in ways that emphasized the virtues, educational systems across the spectrum might follow suit more rapidly.

The formula for teaching virtues we describe in this book works equally well when teaching college classes, though perhaps a stronger emphasis on application of virtues in more advanced contexts than on awareness or development of virtues would prevail. A wonderful model for this is Alverno College, a small woman's college in Milwaukee, Wisconsin, widely respected for its curriculum and assessment innovations. The Alverno curriculum requires all students to demonstrate a mastery of eight abilities that show that they can do something with their knowledge to make the world a better place. These abilities include communication, problem solving and analysis, valuing in decision making, social interaction, global perspectives, effective citizenship, and aesthetic responsiveness. These abilities all interact with core universal virtues and relate specifically to course contexts that draw on them and require them for practical applications.

For example, the ability to develop a global perspective addresses the following levels during the four-year degree program. In level one, students assess what they know about themselves and the world and identify ways to explore the points of connection with earth's biotic and abiotic components.[1] In level two, students use course concepts to examine the relationships among global systems. In level three, students apply their knowledge of global connectedness within the framework of the specific discipline, showing how such connectedness affects the discipline. Level four requires students to use the knowledge and skills they previously acquired to analyze and interpret a topic, drawing on scholarly work and reflection to describe their own perspectives. In level five, students evaluate theoretical strategies to examine a topic related to the course that has global significance. In level six, students are assessed on their ability to determine possible courses of action based on their personal and professional understanding of the global aspects regarding the topic.

To make these complex abilities teachable, Alverno articulates each one as a series of developmental levels corresponding to student progress *across the college career of each student*. A student might pass a course in American history, but still need work on some level to attain one or more of the abilities. This need is recorded and passed on to a subsequent teacher for evaluation in another course. This integrative assessment approach emphasizes the importance of these abilities in all subjects. By using our Pedagogy and Procedures Checklist and maintaining a focus on the virtues, any college can use the Alverno model as an ideal basis for reforming institutions of higher learning. (By the way, Alverno is one of the few colleges in the United States that does *not* use a letter grading system. People come from all over the world to study Alverno's assessment model.)

Teacher Preparation Programs in Higher Education

In our opening chapters, we said that teacher preparation programs around the country have not been training teachers to implement character education effectively across the curriculum. It is worth reviewing the problem briefly here. In *Character Education: The Foundation for Teacher Education*, Emily Nielsen Jones reports research findings based on data from 600 teacher education programs nationally. The programs were selected randomly from 1,326 four-year teacher education institutions. In her chapter, "How Character Education Fares in Teacher Education," she presents the following conclusions:[2]

1. There is overwhelming support for the concept of character education but little implementation.
2. Only 6.6 percent said character education was highly emphasized.
3. There is little philosophical consensus about what character education is and how it should be taught, though most agree with an "across the curriculum" mandate.
4. Religious schools of education are more focused on character education than nonreligious schools.[3]
5. State commitments to character education received low marks.

With these shortcomings in mind, our traditional approach to teaching virtues across the curriculum can remedy this sad picture.

Civic Learning in Higher Education

Another way to incorporate teaching virtues into higher education that is gaining recognition around the world is referred to as *civic learning*. It aims to prepare all college students, faculty, staff and administration to become more caring and responsible citizens of local and global communities. Considering that many or most colleges are ripe with overly competitive, divisive, and territorial issues that overshadow virtuous conduct, this is as challenging as a more fundamental transformation in character education per se. However, civic learning may have more momentum behind it as we enter the new millennium than does "character education" per se.

This year, Oglala Lakota College was selected as one of ten pioneering universities to study and pilot "Civic Learning for Higher Education" programs. One of the reasons OLC was chosen has to do with its education department's strong commitment to teaching virtues across the curriculum and OLC's mission, as described on page seven in the introduction of its 1998 Self-Study Report for North Central Accreditation.

> The Lakota perspective is a worldview which derives from the oral creation story of the Lakota people and is, therefore, a living, dynamic view handed down from generation to generation. At the base of this view is an unchanging adherence to the humanistic values of respect, generosity, wisdom, fortitude, bravery and humility. To see the world from the Lakota perspective is to understand that one must live each day guided by these values . . . [These] Lakota values guide all activities at Oglala Lakota College.

This connection between virtues and improved civic engagement is stated clearly in *Civic Responsibility and Higher Education*:

> Although this volume focuses on civic responsibility, we include moral responsibility because we believe the two are inseparable. Because civic responsibility is inescapably threaded with moral values, we believe that higher education must aspire to foster both moral and civic maturity and must confront educationally the many links between them.[4]

Administrators, school board members, influential citizens of the community, and parents are likely to have spent some time on university campuses, so any effort to infuse virtue education (as presented it in this book) into college life and its curricular objectives will go a long way toward helping K–12 schools teach virtues. Colleges are the last place where young people land with open minds before they enter the world of corporate compliance and materialistic priorities. If these institutions of higher education can make a genuine commitment to practices, environments, attitudes, and curriculum that reflect the moral imperative behind civic learning, it will be a significant boon to genuine character education for younger children.

In many ways it is a "chicken or egg" question to ask whether teaching virtues is best started in higher education or in lower schools. Ultimately, perhaps the answer is both. What is most important is that everyone who talks about the importance of education and the appropriateness of facilitating the road to good character also makes a sincere and courageous commitment to doing something about it. We close this chapter with David Purpel's expression of this idea: "Above all else, we need a language of moral vision and commitment. Moral education without affirmation and commitment is a contradiction in terms, an evasion, and an act of irresponsibility."[5]

Notes

1. This is from a draft of Alverno's description of its program as last modified in May 1999 and given as a handout during a recent Civic Learning conference in which Oglala Lakota College and Alverno are partnership universities.

2. Jones, October 1999, p. 47–48.

3. Unfortunately, this may or may not correlate with universal virtues in schools that emphasize only religious orthodoxy and nonuniversal values with punitive-based compliance with the authority of a specific church.

4. Colby et al., 2000, p. xxiv.

5. Purpel, 2000, p. 254.

The Beginning

You are in this universe and this universe is in you.
— Joy Harjo, Creek Indian poem, from *Secrets from the Center of the World*

There is no alternative to ultimate happiness other than the spiritual way.
We must make a strong determination to practice.
— The XIV Dalai Lama, *Holistic Education Review*

Any education worthy of its name is essentially education of character.
— Martin Buber, *I and Thou*

These last few words are not so much a conclusion as they are a reminder about new beginnings. The previous pages have presented a simple, expedient way to show teachers and students how to walk into a future illuminated by the core universal virtues that have been the beacon of North American Indian people for thousands of years. Guided by such virtues, we immersed ourselves into life's joys and sufferings without losing sight of Nature's "beauty above, below and all around."* Sadly, the dominant culture continues to bury this perspective under a heap of promises and pollution. Its beacon seems to point the way toward an economic reality that disregards virtues as it ignores our other vital resources. Moreover, few of our institutions sufficiently address this misdirection. Only a genuinely spiritual way of life based on courage, generosity, patience, fortitude, humility, honesty and a genuine awareness of our vast and intricate interconnections can bring us back on the "chanku luta." (This translates as "red road" but means a path of health and balance.)

As we have learned, these virtues that cross all boundaries cannot be "taught" in isolation. They are woven into all subjects that are worth learning. Such teaching begins by remembering that our children are sacred. When we remember this, those of us who may have temporarily lost our patience, humility, or our courage are likely to regain these and other virtues in daily thoughts and actions. New teachers, emerging from teacher preparation schools that themselves lack in the virtues education across the curriculum perspective, can also start anew in the classroom with our approach. With the teaching virtues across the curriculum priority in mind, and with the commitment to "walking the talk," we can finally turn school renewal rhetoric into reality.

We offer many thanks for your participation in this project and, for the sake of All Our Relations, we wish you a healthy and joyous life. Do not hesitate to call on us if we can offer further assistance.

Don Jacobs and Jessica Jacobs-Spencer
September 2000

(Note: The authors are available for presenting dynamic, interactive workshops. They can be contacted through Scarecrow Education, by visiting TeachingVirtues.net, or by emailing the authors at *wahinkpe@yahoo.com*. Continuing Education Credits or university credit hours may be receiving for this training through Oglala Lakota College and other participating universities.)

*This phrase is from a Navajo Earth Spirit Prayer, "It is all in Beauty,"

Bibliography

Abram, David. *Spell of the Sensuous*. New York: Vintage, 1996.

Allen, Tom. *Manager as Warrior*. Sioux Falls, S.D.: Sinte Gleska University Press, 1993.

Amundson, Kristen J. *Teaching Values and Ethics: Problems and Solutions*. Arlington,Va.: American Association of School Administrators, 1991.

Bartlett, John, comp. *Familiar Quotations*, 9th ed. Boston: Little, Brown & Co., 1901. *www.bartleby.com*.

Bowers, C. A. *Educating for an Ecologically Sustainable Culture: Rethinking Moral Education, Creativity, Intelligence and Other Modern Orthodoxies*. Albany: State University of New York, 2000.

Boyer, Ernest L. *College: The Undergraduate Experience in America*. Princeton, N.J.: Carnegie Foundation for the Advancement of Teaching, 1982.

————. *The Basic School: A Community of Learners*. Princeton, N.J.: Carnegie Foundation for the Advancement of Teaching, 1995.

Brendtro, Larry K., Martin Brokenleg, and Steve Van Bockern. *Reclaiming Youth at Risk*. Bloomington, Ind.: National Educational Service, 1990.

Brewer, M. B., and W. D. Crano. *Social Psychology*. Minneapolis, Minn.: West Educational Publishers, 1999.

Brown, John Seely, and Paul Duguid. *The Social Life of Information*. Cambridge, Mass.: Harvard Business School Press, 2000.

Buber, Martin. *I and Thou*. New York: Charles Scribner's Sons, 1970.

Burns, Marilynn. *About Teaching Mathematics*. Sausalito, Calif.: Math Solutions Publishers, 2000.

Byers, Paul. "The Spiritual in the Classroom." *Holistic Education Review* (Spring 1992).

Caine, R. N., and G. Caine. *Education on the Edge of Possibility*. Alexandria,Va.: Association for Supervision and Curriculum Development, 1997.

Cajete, Gregory. *Look to the Mountain: An Ecology of Indigenous Education*. Durango, Colo.: Kivaki Press, 1994.

California State Department of Education, "The Making of a New Nation: The Role of Broken Treaties." In *California History and Social Science Standards, 5.3, #4* at *http://www.cde.ca.gov/board/*.

Chesterton, G. K. "Negative and Positive Morality." *Illustrated London News*, London, U.K., January 3, 1920.

Clifton, James A. *The Invented Indian: Cultural Fictions and Government Policies*. New Brunswick, N.J.: Transaction Books, 1990.

Cline, H. F., and R. F. Feldmesser. *Program Evaluation in Moral Education*. Princeton, N.J.: Educational Testing Service, 1983.

Colby, Anne, Thomas Ehrlich, with E. Beaumont, J. Rosner, and J. Stephen. "Higher Education and the Development of Civic Responsibility." In T. Ehrlich (ed.), *Civic Responsibility and Higher Education*. Phoenix, Ariz.: American Council on Education, Oryx Press, 2000.

Colorado Senate Bill 114. In *http://www.rmfc.org/bills.html#Sbills*, October 1999.

Council for Global Education. *Excellence in Character Series*. Washington, D.C., 1997.

Dalai Lama, "Education and the Human Heart." *Holistic Education Review* 10(3) (August 1997): 6.

Deloria, Vine, Jr. *American Indians, American Justice*. Austin: University of Texas Press, 1983.

―――. "Western civilization" quoted in *http://www.indians.org/welker/vine.htm*, November 17, 2000.

DeRoche, Edward F., and Mary M. Williams. *Educating Hearts and Minds: A Comprehensive Character Education Framework*. Thousand Oaks, Calif.: Corwin Press, Inc., 1999.

Dewey, John. *Human Nature and Conduct: An Introduction to Social Psychology*. New York: Random House, 1930.

Diamond, Stanley. *The Search for the Primitive*. New Brunswick, N.J.: Transaction Books, 1974.

Ehrlich, Thomas. *Civic Responsibility and Higher Education*. Phoenix, Ariz.: Oryx Press, 2000.

Flinchbaugh, Robert W. *The 21st Century Board of Education*. Lancaster, Penn.: Technomic Publishing, 1993.

Freire, Paulo. *Pedagogy of the Oppressed*, New York: Continuum Press, 1999.

Fuchs, Estelle, and Robert J. Havighurst. *To Live on This Earth: American Indian Education*. Albuquerque: University of New Mexico Press, 1972.

Glasser, William. *Schools without Failure*. New York: Harper & Row, 1969.

Goleman, D. *Emotional Intelligence*. New York: Bantam, 1996.

Guerin,G. R., and A. S. Maier. *Informal Assessment in Education*. Palo Alto, Calif.: Mayfield Publishing, 1983.

Harjo, Joy. *Secrets from the Center of the World*. Tucson: University of Arizona Press, 1989.

Herman, J. L., P. R. Aschbacher, and L. Winters. *A Practical Guide to Alternative Assessment*. Alexandria, Va.: Association for Supervision and Curriculum Development, 1992.

Jacobs, Don. *Happy Exercise: An Adventure into a Fit World*. Mountain View, Calif.: Anderson World, Inc., 1981.

―――. *Patient Communication for First Responders: The First Hour of Trauma*. Englewood Cliffs, N.J.: Brady-Prentice-Hall, 1991.

―――. *The Bum's Rush: The Selling of Environmental Backlash (Phrases and Fallacies of Rush Limbaugh)*. Boise, Idaho: Legendary Publishing, 1994.

―――. *Primal Awareness: A True Story of Survival, Transformation and Awakening with the Raramuri Shamans of Mexico*. Rochester, Vt.: Inner Traditions International, 1998.

Jones, Emily Nielsen. "Preview: How Character Education Fares in Teacher Education." In Mary M. Williams and Eric Schaps (eds.). *Character Education: The Foundation for Teacher Education*, Washington: Character Education Partnership, 1999.

Kessler, Rachael. *The Soul of Education: Helping Students Find Connection, Compassion, and Character at School*. Alexandria,Va.: Association for Supervision and Curriculum Development, 2000.

Kohl, Herbert. *Basic Skills*. New York: Bantam, 1984.

Kohlberg, Lawrence. *The Philosophy of Moral Development: Moral Stages and the Idea of Justice*. San Francisco: Harper & Row, 1981.

Kohn, Alfie. "How Not to Teach Values: A Critical Look at Character Education." *Phi Delta Kappan. http://www.alfiekohn.org/teaching/hnttv.htm*, 1997.

Lambert, Linda. *Building Leadership Capacity in Schools*. Alexandria,Va.: Association of Supervisors and Curriculum Development, 1998.

Lawrence, D. H. *Studies in Classical American Literature*. New York, Penguin Books, 1971.

Lewis, C., E. Schaps, and M. Watson. "Beyond the Pendulum: Creating Challenging and Caring Schools." *Phi Delta Kappan* 76(7), 1995.

Mander, Jerry. "How Cyberculture Deletes Nature." *Earth Island Journal* (Winter 1997).

Mann, Horace. *Lectures on Education.* Boston: William B. Fowler, 1845.

Marker, G., and H. Mehlinger. "Social Studies." In P. W. Jackson (ed.). *Handbook of Research on Curriculum.* New York: Macmillan, 1992.

McLuhan, T. C. *Touch the Earth.* New York: Outerbridge & Dienstfray, 1971.

Merleau-Ponty, Maurice (trans. By Colin Smith). *Phenomenology of Perception.* London: Routledge and Kegan Paul, 1962.

Mountain Dreamer, Oriah House. *Dreams of Desire.* Toronto, Canada: Mountain Dreaming, 1995.

Mumford, Louis. "Technics and the Nature of Man." In C. Mitcham and R. MacKey (eds.). *Philosophy and Technology.* New York: Free Press, 1972.

Nabokov, Peter. *Native American Testimony: A Chronicle of Indian-White Relations from Prophesy to the Present. 1492–1992.* New York: Penguin, 1992.

Palmer, Parker. *To Know as We Are Known.* San Francisco: Harper, 1993.

———. *The Courage to Teach.* San Francisco: Jossey-Bass Publishers, 1998.

Peat, F. David. *Blackfoot Physics: A Journey into the Native American Universe.* London: Fourth Estate, 1994.

Pritchard, I. "Character Education: Research Prospects and Problems." *American Journal of Education* 96 (August 1988): 469–493.

Purpel, David E. "Moral Education." In David A. Gabbard (ed.). *Knowledge and Power in the Global Economy: The Politics and Rhetoric of School Reform.* Mahwah, N.J.: Lawrence Erlbaum Associates., Inc., 2000.

Radin, Paul. *Primitive Man as Philosopher.* New York: D. Appleton, 1927.

Rusnak, Timothy. *An Integrated Approach to Character Education.* Port Chester, N.Y.: National Professional Resources, 1998.

Russell, Bertrand. *The Problems of Philosophy.* London: Oxford University Press, 1959.

Slattery, Patrick. *Curriculum Development in the Postmodern Era.* New York: Garland Publishing, 1995.

Sprinthall, Richard. *Educational Psychology: A Developmental Approach.* New York: McGraw Hill, 1998.

Steele, Claude M. "Thin Ice." *Atlantic Monthly* 284 (2) (August 1999).

Sternberg, Robert J. *Thinking Styles.* Cambridge, Mass.: Cambridge University Press, 1997.

Swisher, Karen. "American Indian Learning Styles Survey: An Assessment of Teachers' Knowledge." *Journal of Educational Issues of Language Minority Students* (Spring 1994).

Trungpa, Chongyam. *Shambhala: Sacred Path of the Warrior.* Boston, Mass.: Shambhala Publications, 1995.

Ulam. S. M. *Adventures of a Mathematician.* New York: Charles Scribners' Sons, 1976.

VillaVerde, Leila. "Arts Education." In David A. Gabbard (ed.). *Knowledge and Power in the Global Economy: The Politics and Rhetoric of School Reform.* Mahwah, N.J.: Lawrence Erlbaum Associates., Inc. 2000.

Wink, Joan. *Critical Pedagogy.* New York: Longman, Inc., 2000.

Wood, Chip. *Time to Teach, Time to Learn: Changing the Pace of School.* Greenfield, Mass.: Northeast Foundation for Children, Inc., 1999.

About the Authors

Don Trent Jacobs, head of the Education Department at Oglala Lakota College, has written ten other books, including *The Bum's Rush: The Selling of Environmental Backlash*; *Patient Communication for First Responders*; and *Primal Awareness: A True Story of Survival, Awakening and Transformation with the Raramuri Shamans of Mexico*. Of Cherokee/Muscogee/Scot-Irish ancestry, he is a Lakota sundancer and was given the name *Wahinkpe Topa* (Four Arrows) by esteemed Lakota medicine man Rick Two Dogs. Dr. Jacobs has doctorates in health psychology and curriculum and instruction.

Jessica Jacobs-Spencer teaches eighth-grade mathematics and is a wife and mother in Arcata, California. Her master's degree is in mathematics education. Jessica has participated in a variety of equestrian, kayaking, diving, and sailing adventures with her father, and currently practices gymnastics and martial arts with her husband and son.

About the Contributors

Edwin J. Dawson is an education and research consultant and former director of research and assessment at Oglala Lakota College in South Dakota. He is also a communication consultant for organizations and political candidates. His research interests include educational assessment methodologies, health promotion and disease prevention campaigns, and the use of multimedia educational technologies in asynchronous learning environments. He co-authored *Human Communication* and a number of published and submitted scholarly chapters and articles. Dr. Dawson is also a faculty member at the National Judicial College in Reno, Nevada. He received his Ph.D. in communication from the University of Arizona and his M.A. from the University of Nebraska.

Richard M. Jones has lived on the Pine Ridge Indian Reservation for the past 20 years. He taught seventh- and eighth-grade science at Pine Ridge Elementary School from 1981 to 1986. After spending a year on the Navajo Reservation as a special education teacher, he returned to Pine Ridge to work at Little Wound School as the special education director. He has also worked as a psychological examiner, curriculum specialist, technology mentor, and assistant superintendent of schools. Currently he is a professor in the education department at Oglala Lakota College and is working on a book concerning school boards and whole school reform.